Presents

Monica Grant's

The Ragga
&
The Royal

Published by
THE X PRESS, 55 BROADWAY MARKET, LONDON E8 4PH.
TEL: 081 985 0797

Distributed by Turnaround, 27 Horsell Road, London N5 1XL
Tel: 071 609 7836

Printed and bound in Great Britain

This book is dedicated to Okay-yahs and Yardies wherever their yard may be.

CHAPTER 1

I t was the longest, deepest sleep, with the strangest of dreams. This is the story of Leroy Massop's dream...

Leroy Massop woke up on this particular day feeling great about being black. And feeling great was great. He loved being black and he wanted the world to know it. It was hard to explain and he couldn't put it into words, yet he wanted to shout it out loud. To Leroy, being black meant no worries and that everything was level vibes. No matter what the situation, no matter how bad or how sad, he always felt better for being black. Black meant laughter, joy, happiness, eternal fulfilment and love. It meant you knew you had soul. Being black was beautiful, which meant you were beautiful. Black is that which was first, the original man — millions of years of durability, continuity, permanence. Being black meant dreaming of great ancestors who walked in temples of glory. Even when black meant misery and pain, blackness remained regal, radiant. Being black meant putting more meaning into his life, more meaning into living and loving. Black meant family, helping your sister and brother and loving one another... Being black also meant being African, no matter where you came from, no matter your complexion.

Leroy pulled out the roll of notes held together with a rubber band and flicked through it with a pleasing smile. There was almost five grand there. It was his cut from the weekend jungle rave he had organised up country. It had been a massive success, pure roadblock – sensational. Everybody had had a good time and all his crew got paid, so everybody was happy. He felt no way that the lion's share of the profits had gone to him either, after all the 'banker' always gets paid most. Leroy held the wad under his nose and sniffed... 'Aaaagh!' nothing smelt good like cash. Cash was king and in the world of money, five grand in twenties and fifties was well-respected royalty. He kissed the wad briefly before tucking it back into the black leather money belt he always wore.

Leroy glanced down at his Rolex. He still had an hour before he had to be out at the airport. He pressed down the gas a bit further and cruised effortlessly along the wide road at a steady fifty. That was what he liked about his recently acquired, dark blue BMW 3-series convertible — still gleaming in its newness, it's interior still smelling of fresh upholstery — it made good time in the inner city and on the motorway. He could make it to Gatwick in an hour, which would give him more than enough time to first open up the office and then let his secretary in.

Unusual for a man who is considered a 'good catch' by women, Leroy — the original 'tall, dark and handsome', lean and clean with baby dreadlocks — had little time for the opposite sex even though Patsy, his woman, spent long periods overseas in her air hostess job. Even though women raved about "this really black breddah with the steel-grey eyes" and the "cool an' deadly" smile, Leroy had yet to stray, but dutifully conserved his passions and his energies until the woman he loved returned from her travels. He had heard women say, "you look just like Omar" so many times that it no longer made him swell-headed. Besides, he had more important things to do with his time than behaving like a stud all over London. He preferred making dollars so much that it sometimes clashed with his commitments regarding his woman. Like last night, he almost didn't listen to the answering machine when he staggered home, late. The message had been on the machine for three days — the three days Leroy had been up in Manchester for the marathon 'Jungle Rave' weekend.

"Hi Lee, it's me..."

The voice of his woman beeped out of the answering machine, coming long distance.

"...How are you doing? I'm in Barbados, it's four o'clock on Thursday afternoon and I'm just ringing to tell you that I'll be landing at Gatwick at midday on Monday morning. I'll be on Flight 192 at the South Terminal. Don't forget to pick me up. I hope you're eating well and taking care of your stomach ulcer... Lots of love."

It was a good job that he'd listened to the machine. It would have been embarrassing otherwise and not the first time he had done a 'no-show'. He had got out of it last time by the skin of his teeth, only by vowing that he would never leave her waiting in vain again. And he could feel the pressure, however slight, it was there alright; not just for getting to the airport, but for getting to the airport on time.

Why couldn't Patsy face the facts of life? He was a businessman and that was the way it was. With things going on the way they were — the cost of living getting dreader and dreader, the rich getting richer and the poor getting poorer... he had to make sure that they didn't end up poorer, if they were going to take the step of moving in together and starting a family. "It is the first duty of every man not to be poor," his father had always told him. He had to make some dollars and to make some dollars he had to make some sacrifices. Nobody ever became rich without making sacrifices. He had read several 'get rick quick' books with titles like *How To Become Extremely Rich* and *Why Should White Guys Have All The Fun* and it really did seem like behind every successful man there was a supportive and understanding woman. Patsy had to support him and understand that he didn't always have time to devote to their relationship.

The only way to success was through hard, hard work and plenty of faith. If he worked hard he could one day be extremely rich and wouldn't have to go out hustling. He planned to retire at 35 and from then onwards he would spend all his time with Patsy on a private island in the Caribbean where they would live happily ever after. But until then she had to cool and understand that the business needed him more than she did. Like it or not, trying to make it rich included enduring long hours and not being able to do loads of things that Patsy wanted to do. He wanted to do those things too, but not just now, not just when his dream was close to becoming reality.

Leroy twisted his baby locks absent-mindedly. He admired himself in his rearview mirror and flashed a gold-toothed grin. He looked cool in the latest model Ray-Bans his cousin had sent him from New York. Apparently these wraparound darkers were the popular choice amongst all the bad bwoys over Stateside and now he was the first person in West London with a pair — wicked!

Leroy eased on the brakes lightly and glided the car in the direction of the tube station — where the road was more congested as the block of shops on either side attracted a casual but steady flow of trade. He felt good. At 29-years-old, Leroy Massop was in the prime of his life. He had mapped out his future years ago and was now firmly en route down the grand highway to success. He was a winner and had the potential to become one of the most successful black businessmen out there. All he needed now was that one big break. As far as he was concerned, nothing was going to stand between him and that pot of gold at the end of the rainbow.

"West London belongs to me," he said to himself confidently as he eased his car into the heart of the Grove.

The long-standing Afro-Caribbean community in the Ladbroke Grove, Westbourne Park and Notting Hill areas earned little change from the 'streets paved with gold' which had lured them from the greener pastures of home all those years ago. Leroy thought about it as he slowed the German car to a near-crawl, scanning both sides of the streets for anyone who knew him as he approached the flyover. He was never sure whether he particularly liked the Grove or not. On the one hand the area made you proud to be black, but on the other hand it was a poignant reminder that after fifty years the Afro-Caribbean community had achieved little of its potential in England.

After the great 'liberation' battles of the fifties when the teddy boys had taken a beating, the black community had secured for itself one square mile in north-west London which now boasted the best annual Caribbean street festival in Europe. But what the black residents had gained with the Notting Hill Carnival, they had lost in the battle of economics. Others now controlled the area, having carved out a large chunk of the trade (legal, less legal and downright illegal) for themselves. The Asian off-licences were thriving businesses, especially at Carnival when Mr Singh on the Grove has been known to sing 'tra-la-la-la-lee' gleefully in his Sikh language as revellers gasping for relief from the hot, sticky celebrations formed a hundred-yard queue outside his shop. Middle-income whites had also moved into the area in droves, having picked up homes that were going for a song when the North Kensington neighbourhood was still thought of as 'rough'. Even the impregnable All Saints Road — frontline for many famous last stands of the black struggle — was now home to assorted yuppie bijou designer shops. But after half a century there was little sign of black economic achievement. 'What the raas is going on?' Leroy wondered as the BMW rolled forward. Why did it

6

always seem like the black community were skylarking? 'How come we only own one bookstore, a couple of record stores and pattie shops in the area?' After half a century, how come so few of the community owned their own houses? Now when he thought about it, Leroy couldn't quite remember how things had changed so fast. It wasn't all that long ago that a white boy who accidently found himself on the frontline was guaranteed to take some licks and kicks on behalf of his race.

'We always give up too easily', Leroy thought, looking around him as he eased the car forward at a crawl, in order to pose a little.

So many members of the community were content to conform to the lot they had been given in life; believing they were powerless to take any effective control of their lives. All Leroy had to do was take a look around him; both sides of the road were dotted with pitiful, able-bodied men and women who had allowed the winds of circumstance to blow them in every direction until they finally succumbed to the devil in one of his many guises and now — humiliated by poverty — simply drifted along in life, hoping that something positive would turn up or at least that nothing negative did. There was no longer a sparkle in their eyes or an eagerness for life. What had happened to the hopes, dreams and aspirations they had brought with them when they arrived in Britain on the S.S. Empire Windrush all those years ago? Where were the men and women they could have been? If only they could sever the shackles which held them captive to the bookie shop, dreaming that, "one day, I'll strike it rich, one day my ship will come in."

Leroy kept his BMW cruising easy with a delicate touch of his foot on the accelerator. He felt his money belt for the wad of banknotes again and pulled it out for another quick look. 'Damn!' it was five thousand pounds. The most money he had ever made in three days. He had dreamt so much about all the things he would do if he had that amount of money that he didn't have to spend on anything else. This was pure, raw cash — the genuine article, no credit cards, no flim-flam. He smiled a proud smile to himself. Yes, he had the money now, but those dreams, those carefully thought out plans about how he was going to spend it seemed so far away. He already had a nice car and 'nuff of the latest clothes courtesy of Karl Kani. What else could he do with £5,000? Sure, he could go on a long holiday, but like he was always telling Patsy, he didn't have the time to leave the business to run itself. He was on a successful roll and becoming seriously large out there. Now wasn't the right time to go chillin' and cold maxin' on the coast. In a couple of years, he would be successful enough to employ 'nuff people to run the company, but right now he needed to be there twenty-four-sevens if that was what it took. He tucked the money back in his belt and tooted his horn loudly a couple of times, for no good reason, as the car rolled forward.

Leroy had long vowed not to allow the bullshit in this country to beat him down as it had done his father. Instead, he always held his head high, his back straight and his chest puffed out and walked tall, acted tall, talked big and conducted himself big. He felt he could achieve anything and become anybody he wanted to be. And he would succeed, because he was tenacious, worked hard and had a sense of destiny that one day he would be rich, famous and powerful. He had his eyes fixed firmly on the prize.

That's why he enjoyed modelling in his new sports car, it was a status symbol to every black youngster that they too could make it. Leroy was proud of his car because like he was himself, it was flash and powerful. His cars had always been flash and clean ever since he was a youth... Even that first £50 Ford Anglia which he had turned into a street rod when he was a teenager, with wide tyres, a jacked up rear and the flame-like design on both sides. Like most black youth with flash cars in those days, he was often pulled by the police for no good reason and given a 'producer' (an instruction to appear at the police station within seven days with his insurance, MOT and licence documents). Sometimes he would get pulled two or three times every week. It soon got tiresome and on one occasion he had had to teach a particularly aggressive officer some manners. They had ended up wrestling in the gutter. The charge of assaulting an officer was later dropped before it got to the magistrate's court. Fortunately since then, he had learned the trick of using the police to his benefit and now — as a respected up and coming businessman with a high community profile — the police were more likely to salute him than pull him over.

Poverty wasn't a virtue in Leroy's view, but a vice that could lead to apathy. He couldn't stand seeing beggars, because from experience he had learned that there was no such thing as 'something for nothing'. All you needed in life was a plan, a road map and the courage to press on to your destination with persistence and determination. "Start where you are with what you have, knowing that what you have is plenty enough," his father had always told him. Though there were no short cuts, anything the mind could conceive and believe, it could achieve. All you needed was the right mental attitude.

A few youths standing outside the underground station recognised the ever well-dressed driver of the BMW and pumped up their fists in salute. Leroy tooted his horn loudly and raised his fist high, turning only briefly to acknowledge them. It took an even briefer moment for the elderly black man standing by the traffic lights on the crossing to fall in the road.

Everything happened in a flash. Leroy's subconscious registered the man dressed in a suit and battered trilby that looked like the very clothes the man was wearing when he had stepped ashore from the S.S. Windrush over forty years before. In the same instance, he saw the man's hands reaching to his face for protection. He heard the scream of a passer by...!!

Everything else went as if in slow motion. Sweating profusely from the morning sun blazing through the windscreen, Leroy somehow remembered seeing the anxious faces of passers-by, and recalled pushing the foot pedal all the way down and stopping with a screech of his tyres, just in time...

"Lawd, him kill Robbie! Laaaawd!!!"

The cry chilled Leroy's heart. 'Shit,' he thought, 'if the man's dead... shit!'

He climbed out of the car fast, still in a daze.

"De bwoy kill Robbie, dead! Lawd, somebody run go call police!"

Leroy glared at the screaming man, but decided against throwing an insult. The by-stander and his two companions, each clutching a half-empty bottle of Dragon stout, were senior citizens and if nothing else, respect was due.

At the front of the car, the elderly man lay on the tarmac, spread-eagled on his back. He looked up at his friends standing over him, then at Leroy looking good and dressed fancily — the Rolex, the Ray-Bans, the Armani suit, the Bally's on his feet — then back to his friends.

"Yes, de bwoy try tek my life!" he confirmed, in a high-pitch whine.

Leroy bent down to offer assistance.

"Leggo me hand!" the injured man cried, aiming the walking stick in his hand at Leroy's head and only missing narrowly.

Caught off guard, Leroy stumbled back, the strong smell of alcohol intoxicating him momentarily.

It was then that everything flashed back to him. He had only been driving at a crawl — 15 mph at the most — and he had definitely stopped the car in time. He was sure of it. The car had stopped with the man still standing... then suddenly the man had fallen down. Leroy cast a suspicious eye over the man. His clothes seemed intact — dishevelled, but intact nevertheless. And apart from being a little worse for alcohol, the man seemed alright.

By now a crowd had gathered around the incident. A queue of honking cars had also formed behind the BMW blocking the road, with irate drivers throwing insults.

"Hey bwoy, yuh 'ave licence?" asked the loud-mouthed friend.

"What you talking about?" Leroy demanded.

"Yuh 'ave nice car, but what about licence? Ah who 'llow you fe drive?"

And so it went on for a few minutes... with the old man lying on the road claiming he had been 'killed' and with his drinking buddies hanging tight to Leroy's arm and accusing him of murder! The crowd also took sides against Leroy, with people muttering about "flash bastards in flash cars... think they own the bloody place... you need to get your eyes tested mate, why can't you look where you're bloody driving...? He mowed him down, he did, bloody mowed him down... the old bloke didn't stand a chance."

Leroy even heard someone suggest, "he must be a drugs-dealer driving a car like that." But he spun round to scan the sea of faces surrounding him too late to catch the person who had mentioned it. Leroy looked at his watch again, time was running and running and running. He had to make it to the airport or bust.

Eventually the old man let out a cry from his prostrate position on the ground.

"Somebody call police quick, before him run 'way!"

'Police', that was the one thing Leroy didn't need right now, and the old man and his friends knew it too. Why, otherwise, had the old man requested the police rather than an ambulance? The young funki dred had too many large rings on his fingers and gold 'cargo' hanging from his neck for an ambulance to take precedence. Leroy looked at his watch, it was 11.00am already. Time was going to be tight, but he reasoned, clearing the customs hall at the airport always added a few minutes to international arrivals, even for cabin crew.

The BMW now made its way swiftly towards Portobello, weaving in and out of traffic and down a couple of back streets. "Damn!" Leroy thought to himself. He had been taken for a sucker. He slammed hard on the dashboard. "Damn!" he repeated, that little skank had cost him a fifty note for the old man *and* each of his two colleagues! He always made a point of knowing all the latest skanks so that he wouldn't be caught out, and he had heard that 'knock down ginger' – where a 'serious' road accident is stage-managed before an unsuspecting driver who is then fleeced of his money under pain of prosecution — was making the rounds.

"Damn!" he repeated again, the second hand seemed to be racing around the face of his Rolex. He would have to slip into the office quickly to let Aisha in and then race down to the airport. It was going to be tight, but if he burned rubber on the motorway he would still make it in time.

It wasn't the £150 that bothered him so much. On any other occasion Leroy would have enjoyed the skank. After all, he was always saying that black people never show enough initiative and the old-timers had shown that they were supreme hustlers who could still hold their own in this day and age. Any other day Leroy would have had to hand it to them, but he couldn't afford the leisure time today.

King Lee Enterprises were situated in Terence Yard, a tiny Victorian cobbled yard, tucked away in the middle of a block with a row of antique shops, at the Notting Hill end of Portobello Road. The yard had been purpose-built for stables a hundred years ago and now housed a trio of business units, each squeezed into one of the converted stables which made up the three sides of the yard. There wasn't a sign that announced his business and Leroy liked it that way. The fewer people who knew what was going on in the building the better. This wasn't just an office with phones for him to keep in contact with vendors and suppliers, it also doubled as a stock room. There was probably £10,000 worth of stock in there at any one time and Leroy was too streetwise to shout out loud about it.

This morning, as the blue BMW purred into the yard, a couple of white youths in baseball jackets and caps, turned and fled, both with a couple of the boxes they had been helping themselves to, under each arm. They ran, anxiously squeezing their way out of the narrow yard through the even narrower gap between the BMW and the wall.

It clicked with Leroy immediately that something was going down and he killed the engine and jumped out of the car all in one go and gave chase instinctively, shouting "Stop thief!" as he did.

The youths legged it swiftly down Portobello Road with their shirt backs full of wind and still clutching tight to their booty. Leroy had little chance of catching them.

The youths disappeared down the maze of council estates that bordered one side of the road, at which point Leroy turned and hurried back to the yard.

By now a couple of the guys from the adjoining

businesses had gathered outside to see what the commotion was all about.

"What are those boxes doing there?" Leroy asked, pointing to the hundred or so plain white shoe boxes neatly piled up outside the front entrance to his unit.

"Don't ask me, mate," Vince, from the graphic designer unit said. "Some bloke backs a van into the yard about half hour ago and asks me to sign for them. Says they're for you and you were supposed to be here at ten."

Shit! Leroy remembered the Nike training shoes that Terry was supposed to be delivering.

"Wasn't Aisha waiting outside here to deal with it?" Leroy asked.

"Isha? Who's that?" Vince asked.

"You know that girl who's been working for me... you've seen her loads of times... the girl with the long hair extensions.."

"No mate, sorry... nobody's been in your place all morning," Vince said as he and his colleague returned to their unit.

Shit again, Leroy thought! Okay, he was late, but Aisha was supposed to be there from ten. If she had been there, the kids wouldn't have been able to swipe the boxes they had made off with. So what if she was only a voluntary work placement help, he was going to give her a bollocking when she arrived anyway. This wasn't the way to do business and she had to learn. If he hadn't arrived when he did, the kids would have probably made off with the whole consignment. Still, at least the trainers were here, that was something. He looked at his watch, it was 11.20. It would only take him

15

a few minutes to carry all the boxes inside the unit and if Aisha hadn't come by then he would leave a note for her and rush to the airport. If he was lucky, the plane would be a few minutes late — after all they usually were — and he would catch Patsy just as she was coming out of the customs hall.

Leroy had been very fortunate to get the deal on the hundred pairs of Nike sneakers. It was rare that street traders like himself ever got a good deal on top of the range training shoes, so this was something of a coup, an irresistible business opportunity. And he had snapped the hundred pairs up almost as soon as Terry, his regular wholesaler, called him on the mobile to tip him off.

"You'll love this stuff, mate," Terry had insisted, "...top of the range stuff... sell 'em anywhere... selling like hot patties all over the place..."

Terry assured Leroy that the training shoes, a consignment of Nike seconds, would fetch a good price on the open market.

"They're in perfect condition," his voice crackled down the line. "I can't understand why they're seconds. I'm wearing a pair myself. Trust me Leroy, they're going to go like hot batties."

"Batties?! You mean patties, innit?"

"Yeah man, that's what I said, hot patties."

"Well, as long as they're not as *hot* as hot patties," Leroy teased.

"Oh come on, man, you know me Leroy, me nah inna dat, star. Strickly legal runnings."

"So watcha dealin'-dealin'?" Leroy asked, getting back to the business at hand.

"A hundred pairs at £10 a pair, a cool grand, I can't take nothing less."

"Well I'm talking £5 a pair," Leroy told Terry. "I can't offer nothing more."

"You've got to be joking, star," came the anxious reply. "This is good stuff, Leroy, or I wouldn't be calling. You'll be able to get thirty quid a pair for them down the high street, maybe more."

Leroy paused, making some quick mental calculations.

"They'd better be good..." he said.

"Take my word for it."

Leroy smiled as he pulled a pair of the trainers out of the box. A good line in trainers would go down very well on the street level, he knew that. Everybody wanted Nikes, they would definitely be easy to sell. With any luck they might be the popular new Air Darwins... Then he caught sight of the label on the sturdy black training shoes.

"What the fuck is this?!" he cried aloud, both in shock and dismay.

'Mike'? What the raas was Mike? He had paid a grand for a hundred pairs of Nike trainers and he had got a hundred pairs of Mike delivered! What the raas was going on?!

Leroy jerked his mobile from his breast pocket and dialled furiously. He knew the number off by heart.

"Terry? Where's Terry, put me through... Tell him it's Leroy..."

He waited, the mobile tight against his ear. There had to be an explanation. He turned the shoe over in his hand again. This had to be some kind of a joke.

17

"Yeah, Lee man," the voice came crackling down the line. "Wha' ah gwan, don man?"

"Terry, you're taking the piss aren't you? Tell me you're taking the piss?"

"Waddap, man? Taking the piss? About what?"

"The trainers man... the trainers...Mike trainers gettit? Not Nikes but Mikes."

Terry didn't seem to be seeing the funny side and simply answered deadpan.

"Yeah, Mikes man, a new name, trust me... all the kids will be wearing 'em soon..."

"Mikes? You told me they were Nikes!"

"No mate, you got that wrong... Mikes is what I said; you ought to get yourself a new phone mate, 'cause yours ain't working too good. Anyways... Mikes, Nikes, what's the difference? They're great shoes, trust me. The kids will love 'em and for £10 a pair, you're laughing...""

"You're kidding me, ain't you mate?"

Leroy refused to see the funny side. There was no way he was going to pay a grand for any training shoes called Mike. Who would buy them? Nobody was going to shell out £30 on a pair of Mike trainers. Terry insisted that he had clearly said Mike, but accepted that it was probably a genuine mistake.

"Do you honestly believe that if they were Nikes I would let you have them for a tenner each? You're the one taking the piss now, Leroy."

Still, in the interest of their long-term friendship and the frequent business between them, Terry offered the shoes to Leroy at a fiver a pair. Leroy offered three. Terry settled for four.

Leroy switched off the phone. He had already made a

mental note of the handsome profit he could make if he sold them for £9.99 a pair. He admired the trainer in his hand once more. Yeah, they didn't look too bad and if you kept a keen price you'd always find takers. He looked at his watch. Shit! 11.40. Patsy, the airport... What should he do? There was no way he was going to get there without being half an hour late. Was it still worth driving down? The memory of the last time he never showed up came back to him, Patsy's threat to forget who he was if he forgot to pick her up again. He had to try to make it. He quickly packed the rest of the boxes inside the unit. Aisha had still not arrived, so he wrote her a message telling her where she could pick up the key.

Finally as 11.50, Leroy climbed back into the BMW, turned the ignition and gunned the engine. He had ten minutes to drive the one hour journey to Gatwick... He eased himself out of Terence Yard in reverse and backed onto Portobello Road, turned the steering and with the wheels straight, raced away in a screech of burning tyre, a fast aggressive junglist track blasting out of the car stereo, as he headed for the airport in great haste.

CHAPTER 2

D ressed in a British Airways cabin crew uniform, Patsy stood outside Gatwick Airport's South Terminal in the blazing midday sun, glancing at her watch impatiently and scanning the constant stream of vehicles that drew up for a sign of Leroy's new BMW. Her flight from Barbados had only just landed and as usual for cabin crew she cleared immigration and customs in no time at all. She was on time, but now at 12.30, there was still no sign of Leroy. She couldn't believe that he wouldn't show up after the way he had dissed her the last time. She didn't think it was too much to ask the man you're having a relationship with to come and pick you up at the airport on your return home from a flight overseas with your job. Especially when he knew how difficult it was to get into town from Gatwick, he could show some old-fashioned romance and have a carriage waiting for his sweetheart, if he really did love her as much as he was always saying. However, after that last time when she had stood waiting for an hour in vain, she had made it clear that she didn't want to be left standing. She didn't mind if he couldn't make it, as long as she knew. Leroy had insisted, as he always did, that there wasn't a thing he wouldn't do for his woman and was she suggesting that he wasn't romantic enough, didn't love her enough? He had vowed that he would pick her up *and* he would be there on time. She had even called from Barbados four days ago to remind him, in case he had forgotten. Leroy had no excuses. She would wait, but if he didn't show, she would make sure that he never forgot it. She carried on looking intently at the continuing flow of cars that were picking up and setting down passengers outside the terminal, but there was still no sign of Leroy.

Everybody had warned Patsy to keep away from Leroy when they first met; her family and friends and even some of *his* family and friends. Her parents were dismayed that their daughter would take up with someone they considered a ragamuffin. "And he is a raggamuffin," her father had said, "just look at his table manners, look at those clothes, the way he talks... and I'm sure he takes drugs!" Jamaican fathers will be Jamaican fathers and Mr Hines had not slaved for thirty years in this country, eventually setting up a successful Jamaican fast food restaurant and managing to send his daughter to a good school, only to see her throw it away on a "no good loafer." What baffled Mr Hines the most about his daughter's choice of boyfriend was that he wasn't even handsome. "...An' yuh see how de bwoy ugly so?" he would ask his wife every night as they lay in bed. Why was Patsy with him? His daughter was attractive and in her teenage days had always had a string of handsome boys running after her. Since then she had matured and become an even more attractive woman. Her short, boyish hair styles always oozed confidence and her figure-hugging skirt suits made her look cool and efficient. Sure she was his daughter, but she had the same melting eyes as her mother and the same sparkling smile that had made him fall in love with her mother thirty years before. So why did she waste her time with this Leroy? Patsy often wondered the same thing. But like as always, rationale and reasoning go out the window when you are in love. Talk didn't mean a single thing when she felt in the mood for love. How could she explain to her friends and family how Leroy made her feel the way she did when she was alone with him, in bed, far away from the hustle and bustle of street life; how he could make her cold nights hot, how he could get her humming, craving for more? Even after he had fallen asleep, she would often stay awake kissing his deep brown skin from belly button to ear lobe, listening to his strong heart beating, playing with every hair on his chest. She loved him so much. There are no guarantees in love, so sometimes it was frightening the way Leroy made her feel, yet it felt good to her. He knew she couldn't resist him, that's the way love goes. But he also knew a different side of her: she was unforgiving when her pride was hurt.

Though to others he might look even more handsome with a nice, short, tidy haircut, Patsy still felt Leroy was good looking in an unconventional sense. And okay, he hadn't been to university, but qualifications weren't everything and she was sure that it wouldn't be long before her father was commending Leroy's entrepreneurial skills. Whatever faults he had, she wasn't interested in checking other men as her girl friends were always suggesting. At 24 years of age she was happy that Leroy was her man; all he had to do was prove that he cared about his woman by showing up at the airport and everything would be sweet.

Patsy sighed and looked at her watch again. The blazing midday sun was wearing her down. Sure, she could jump into one of the many taxis lined up outside the terminal waiting for a fare. It would have been easy. She had so little luggage she could even take the bus. If she had never mentioned being picked up from the airport in the first place, Leroy would never have offered to do it himself to express his love. He was always stressing how much he missed her when she was away for more than a few days. That was the nature of the air hostess job and she had learned to get used to it over the last two years. She had really only applied for the job as a dare with one of her girlfriends, one lazy Sunday afternoon after her finals, when there was little to do but sit in the park and fill in the crossword. To her surprise, she was offered an interview for the job, which went well. Particularly impressive was the fact that her degree had strengthened her proficiency in the two European languages she had been studying since school. Eventually, Patsy became one of only a handful of black air hostesses employed by major British airlines. It was hard work, especially working on the long-haul flights, but the job had given her an opportunity of seeing far away corners of the world she would never have been able to afford to visit on her own. She had been to cities such as Tokyo, Sydney, Buenos Aires, Rio, Moscow, Helsinki, Los Angeles and Bombay, as well as places with exotic names such as Dubai, Jakarta, Kinshasa and the Bahamas. The good thing about the long distance hauls was that after every few days of work, the crew would get a few days rest at one of their destinations. This had given her time to do some sightseeing, have some adventures and get to learn a little bit about the cultures of people far removed from her own. Of all the good times she had had, there was none so enjoyable as being in Johannesburg recently on the day that Nelson Mandela became president of a free South Africa. There Patsy had joined up with a party of young township women she had met outside her hotel and they had spent three days together celebrating the occasion with song and dance.

She looked at her watch again. It was 12.40. She was feeling increasingly impatient and irritated, but decided on giving Leroy another five minutes. Before she departed for her ten days away from home, he had seemed so determined to prove to her that he was responsible enough and cared enough about her and their relationship to be able to pick her up at the appointed arrival time. It was hard to believe that he would diss her again so casually.

Patsy had discussed her new job with Leroy before accepting it. He had insisted that she should do whatever she desired. He honestly didn't mind. But what about their relationship which at the time had only been going a year and was already under some strain? Would it last with her jetsetting all over the world and being away from home a lot? Leroy had insisted that he was crazy about her and the fact that she was away from home wouldn't diminish his feelings. She believed him. As it was, they weren't living together anyway. They had tried it once, at the very beginning of their relationship, to disastrous consequences. The fact that they chose to live apart hadn't affected their relationship negatively. On the contrary, it had probably enhanced and prolonged it. There was no longer the tense vibes they felt when they were permanently under the same roof. Though they maintained the obligations of a formal relationship, they each had their own space in which to meditate in solitude and gather their thoughts together. Friends and family called it 'a modern relationship'.

So Leroy was happy with any decision she made concerning the job. If she was happy, he was happy. Patsy thought about it long and hard before she finally made her decision. What made up her mind more than anything was the realisation that she'd probably not see Leroy any less if she was flying all over the world and coming back every couple of weeks, than if she stayed in London. 'Modern relationships' all good and well, but Leroy had contributed little to the relationship in the preceding six months. His mind was so fully engrossed in his mission to be rich and successful, that he had all but neglected his woman. It was she who was always having to call him and to pressure him into going out or doing something together. He never seemed to be able to find the time. He was always on the move, dealing with his runnings... his jugglings... his deals. It was great that Leroy had ambition and was doing what was necessary to get where he wanted to be in life. She supported him to the maximum, but didn't want him to achieve his ambitions only to change along the way. That seemed to have been what was happening of late. The jovial, amiable, happy-go-lucky Leroy that she had first met more than three years ago, now had a touch of coldness about him. Ambition, it seemed, had made him a less nice person — who had little time for relationships but also felt guilty about contributing very little to the success of their love. One of the reasons Patsy took the job with the airline was that the greater the distance between her and her man, the less he would have to feel guilty about things. It would give him enough time to work on his business plans without her distressing the situation. Leroy kept saying that he needed just a couple of years to get his business flowing nicely and then he would be ready to spend all his time with her. If that was the case then fine, she would give him time, but she wasn't going to hitch her star to the success of Leroy's business, so she maintained a state of perpetual readiness for the ending of their relationship — just in case. She didn't want to be caught out unawares.

She looked at her watch again and sighed helplessly. Still no sign of him. Well, she had given him his chance.

"Excuse me ma'am, you look lost, like you could do with some help. Allow me to offer my services..."

Patsy spun around to face the handsome, smiling features of an elegantly dressed man, the owner of the deep American voice, his hand outstretched and a business card between his fingertips.

"Hi, Joseph R. Reynolds," he said in his slightly gruff yank accent. "Most of my friends call me J.R."

Still taken aback, Patsy glanced at the business card: Joseph R. Reynolds, President, Reynolds Promotions Inc. She couldn't help noticing how dishy the man was. A smooth and stylish, deep-bronze coloured 'man of the nineties' who used Magic Shave rather than a razor, his hair relaxed and slicked back with Dax hair oil into a short, wet-look style, his fingernails manicured, his dark suit immaculate, the rings on his fingers expensive, a pinstripe moustache and a shine on his face. He gave the impression of being a dashing dandy from the pages of Ebony. Not exactly Johnny Gill, but a slightly older and chubbier version.

"I just flew in from New York, first class of course — the only way to fly!" J.R. laughed, self-consciously. "I should have flown on Concorde like I usually do but it doesn't land at Gatwick. Have you ever flown Concorde?"

Patsy sized the man up silently and shook her head.

"You haven't? Believe me, that's the only way to fly. Of course it's all first class, so you get treated really well. The flight's so quick, I hardly ever get a chance for a nap, because four hours later, you're in London. And then when you arrive at the airport, you never get any trouble from Customs and Immigration when you step off Concorde. Not like today... Can you believe that these Immigration guys questioned me for a half hour and then the Customs went through my bags like I had a bomb in there!"

Patsy shrugged her shoulders.

"Yes, something needs to be done about those guys... to teach them some respect for black travellers."

J.R. shrugged his shoulders also. The customs guys were jealous of a black man with some dollars, he concluded.

"Listen, I know it's probably none of my business but is everything alright? You look like you just *dropped* out of the sky."

"No everything is not alright!" Patsy sighed looking at her watch again. Leroy should have been there ages ago. It was unlikely that he was going to show up. She was angry, but didn't want her feelings for her wotless boyfriend to affect her conversation with this interesting American guy. She would deal with Leroy later.

"What's up?" J.R. asked, "did your ride not show up?"

"Something like that. I was crazy to expect him to show up... You know what men are — unreliable!" Patsy said with a half-serious smile.

"Hey please!" J.R. raised his hand in protest. "Don't make judgements about me, when you hardly know me. There are many different types of men and I'm of a type that don't know the meaning of 'unreliable'."

J.R. assured her that there were 'brothers' like himself, who were sensitive and gave as much care, concern and tenderness as they desired from their women. Patsy insisted that she still didn't believe it, so they were deadlocked for a moment.

"Are you going into London, because I'm getting a cab anyway, maybe I could drop you off somewhere?"

Patsy eyed the man for a moment; his well-cut silk suit, the white silk shirt, colourful tie and waistcoat and Italian loafers. She had to admit that he intrigued her. It was the manner in which he conducted himself and the way he talked, as well as the way he made her feel at ease talking to him. What harm could there be? Leroy wasn't going to show up, so she really did need a lift into town.

"That's very kind of you," she replied with a smile. "If you drop me anywhere in town, I'll be able to make my way home more easily."

"My pleasure," JR insisted with a broad smile. "But I wouldn't dream of dropping you off anywhere but outside your home, I insist."

With a confident wave of his hand, Leroy flagged down one of the black cabs that had been constantly circling the airport terminal looking for passengers. He got lucky, it was a black driver for a change, who greeted them with a broad, welcoming smile. J.R. took Patsy's case from her and lifted it with his into the cab, then held the door open for his fellow passenger.

'At least the man's got some manners', Patsy thought, as the taxi rolled off towards London.

If only Leroy had arrived at the airport five minutes earlier. It had taken him over an hour to get there, with the fear of his woman's wrath 'tailgating' him all the way. Even as late as he was, if he had decided on driving directly outside the terminal he could have just made it. But, pressed for time, he reasoned that Patsy would have more likely waited in the Arrivals Hall and therefore he had to drive into the multi-storey car park to leave the car. He raced towards the Arrivals Hall, the seconds ticking away... the time was 1.00pm. Okay, he was nearly an hour late and yeah, Patsy was always impatient, but she could still be waiting... She had to be.

Personally, he didn't see why it was such a big thing for him to be there at the airport to pick her up every time she flew back in, but Patsy did. He felt she could just have easily taken a cab in or the train. It would have been almost as quick and would save him a lot of time that he could ill afford. Time waits for no one. He had his business to be getting on with. He wanted to be rich as much as the hungry man wants bread, as much as the choking man wants air. To become rich he had to seize the time and the opportunities. He had explained to Patsy that he needed to start work early, stay late and work tirelessly in between. "If I see what I want really clearly in my mind, I don't notice any pain in getting it." Self-discipline was the first rule of successful management, even if it meant that you wouldn't always have time for your woman. "Whatsoever a man soweth, that shall he also reap," he would quote her to which she would reply, "If you want love, *give* love!" Leroy had to concede that she had a point with that, but again, he couldn't see how not picking her up from the airport meant that he loved her less, or that he missed her any less. He still loved her, genuinely loved her, like it was in the beginning. He didn't want to lose her. She was the woman of his dreams. He was proud that she was an air hostess, despite having to spend so many nights when she was away with his arms wrapped tightly around a pillow when he would rather have been embracing her. Still, Patsy was soft on the little romantic things. He didn't really understand how much so until he had missed picking her up a couple of times. They had almost split up over that... So here he was at Gatwick Airport.

He scanned the Arrivals Hall to no avail. The information screen displayed that Patsy's flight had landed on time, but there was no sign of her amongst all the newly-arrived and their friends and families. It suddenly struck him that she might be waiting outside, expecting him to just drive up and pick her up.

As he stepped into the terminal's automatic revolving doors leading out, he caught sight of Patsy's unmistakable figure climbing into a black cab followed by some overweight smoothie. "Patsy!" he yelled, banging on the glass door and giving it a hard shove to make it revolve faster. Suddenly the doors came to an abrupt stop. Leroy was trapped in the middle, unable to get either in or out. He pushed harder on the door, frantically, as he saw the taxi pulling away, taking his woman with it. He called out to her once more and pushed harder, using his whole bodyweight in the effort, but no joy, it didn't budge. He saw the taxi pulling away. Still banging on the door, he heard someone cry from behind him:

"Don't touch the doors...!!"

He turned to face a policeman with a bulletproof vest and an automatic rifle. From behind the glass of the revolving doors, Leroy raised his hands instinctively.

"I'm just trying to get out, take it easy. I'm stuck!"

"Then don't touch the doors!" the policeman barked. "It won't move if you touch the doors."

Suddenly it made sense. Leroy remembered that he had been in one of these modern automatic revolving doors before. If you touched the doors, it would stop automatically. He had trapped himself inside.

Leroy stepped back and the doors swung round automatically. He stepped out. He felt shame for his naivety, but more importantly, he felt his stomach ulcer burn... Patsy would never believe that he had missed her because he had knocked someone down and been robbed all in the same morning.

CHAPTER 3

It's amazing how many men are prepared to leave their women at home with lust in their hearts, while they are out attending to their runnings. They keep forgetting that there are more than enough men out there to find their women attractive; men who are only too willing to get these lonely women behind closed doors and give them what they crave. In Patsy's case, the fact that she was an air hostess was an added attraction for a lot of men, not least of all, the handsome and charming J.R. Reynolds.

"So you get to fly all over the world? No kidding?" said J.R. in his particularly effervescent manner. "I bet you've been to some interesting places?"

J.R. had explained that he was in London on business. He was a boxing promoter studying the possibilities of putting on a heavyweight championship fight in London.

"Oh I love boxing," Patsy said enthusiastically, "which boxers are you promoting?"

J.R. wasn't the first yank she'd met and she knew that they were prone to more than a little bullshit. However, she was intrigued by this guy and wanted to find out if he was for real.

J.R. smiled a big and broad smile and puffed up his chest.

"Well, if you promise to keep it a secret," he said.

"Oh of course."

"Well, Mike Tyson's getting out of jail in a few months. I've done a deal with him. I am his sole representative."

Up front, the cab driver's ears pricked up now and he listened to his passengers' conversation with interest. Tyson had been one of his favourite boxers before the system decided to crucify him with a jail sentence. The taxi driver had seen youths over on his side of town sporting the T-shirts with Tyson's face and the motif, 'I'll be back...' It was good to get confirmation that the real heavyweight champion of the world really was making a comeback. Anyway, it wasn't his conversation, so he kept his eyes on the road, heading down the motorway to west London.

Patsy's eyes opened wide. Mike Tyson! The look in J.R.'s face testified to his sincerity.

"So, he's about to get out of jail?"

"Yes, but as I said... it's all hush hush at the moment. This is a billion dollar deal. When Tyson gets out, the whole world's going to want to see him fight... to see if he's still got it in him... a fight like that has got to be worth a billion dollars to somebody, right? But you've got to keep it quiet, I don't want anything messing up my chances. That's why I'm sneaking into London by taxi. Usually the big promoters would have sent a limousine for me."

"So have you met Tyson personally?"

"Met him? We go back a long way, we were at school

together, used to play football and baseball together. Terrible what's happened to him. He's my homeboy and I swear to God he couldn't have done the things they said he did... swear to God. It must have been a set up."

Mike Tyson! Patsy could still hardly believe her ears. So much had been written about the ex-heavyweight champion since he was convicted of date raping that when he made his comeback she, like everybody else, would be glued to a television watching to see if he could regain his former title, and what he looked like after years in jail.

"So tell me..." J.R. suddenly changed tact, "I'm going to be in London for a few days trying to find sponsors. But I have a lot of free time. If you're in town you could maybe show me around."

It was a statement more than a question. J.R. was very confident of himself. 'And why shouldn't he be?', Patsy thought, after all he had the looks and he seemed to have potential.

'This is one fine sister', J.R. thought to himself. 'Even a blind man could look at her and see she was irresistible'.

"I bet you must have a lot of male admirers," he said interestedly, "an attractive woman like you."

" 'Woman shall not live by male admirers alone'."

"So do you have any admirer in particular, a boyfriend? A husband?"

"Why do you ask?"

J.R. was unruffled by the question.

"Oh I noticed that you weren't wearing a wedding ring," he said glancing down at her finger, "and I was wondering whether it was because air stewardesses aren't allowed to wear wedding rings. I think I heard that somewhere?"

"Of course not," Patsy said, "it's because I'm not married."

As soon as she said that, J.R. straightened himself up And raised an eyebrow.

"In that case, if I may say so, you've just found yourself another admirer."

"But I do have a boyfriend... at least I did have before I departed two weeks ago. I'm not too sure if he still wants me, or more to the point if I want him now."

"He's the guy who didn't show up to pick you up?"

Patsy kissed her teeth, she didn't need to answer.

"Well, if you don't mind my saying it, I think he must be a jerk. What kind of a brother is that who leaves his woman standing at the airport after a long flight?"

"He's the kind of 'brother' who cares more about money than he does about his woman," Patsy sighed.

"Damn, what an asshole!" J.R. declared. "I've got money... a lot of money in fact, but that could never be more important than my woman. If you were my woman I would always have to respect you."

"I don't believe that those type of men exist anymore."

"Believe me, there are some nice and decent sensitive men out there, real romantic types who will treat you good. You women just aren't looking in the right places."

Patsy wasn't convinced. She looked out of the taxi window. She didn't know why Leroy hadn't shown up, but she didn't care anymore. They were driving through the outskirts of London now, side by side with the familiar red double decker buses of the capital. The taxi meter had already clocked up many pounds, but that seemed to be the last thing on the American's mind.

"So what about you?" Patsy asked. "With all your charm, I bet you have a different woman in every city? What is it they say, behind every successful man there's got to be a woman."

"Not in my case. Yeah, I've got money in my pocket, but I just can't find a woman with that something special in love..."

J.R. stared out of the window for a moment, reflectively, as the taxi continued its journey into the heart of the city.

"Well who's perfect?" Patsy offered, "I don't know one person who's perfect."

"You're pretty close to perfect," J.R. said quickly turning towards Patsy on the taxi seat beside him. He had wanted to compliment her for most of the journey, but couldn't figure out the best way to tell her what was on his mind. There was something about this sweet English woman that told him to check himself, to take it easy with this one, that she needed a gentle touch. The signs told him that this might still turn out exactly the way he desired if he played his cards right.

"Don't you think you should find out a bit more about me before you make statements like that?" Patsy asked, unimpressed.

J.R. looked deep into her eyes with as much sincerity as the situation warranted.

"Yes, it would help if I got to know you better, but I like what I see already."

"So what is it exactly that you like? You like my

legs?"

"Yes and your arms and your neck, your eyes, your mouth..." J.R, said, moving in close to her.

"But that's just my body. You started off saying I was perfect, now I find out that you don't mean *me* at all, just my body."

Patsy enjoyed this friendly jousting with J.R. She didn't need a shoulder to cry on to get Leroy's let down off her chest, she just needed an ego boost.

When someone laughs and harmonizes with you, you feel you enjoy their company better. Even J.R.'s flattery worked. It didn't matter that she knew she was no more perfect than anybody else, it was just nice to hear kind words after standing waiting for Leroy outside the terminal for an hour and feeling unloved, unwanted and unappreciated. Leroy had never appreciated how easy it was to give his woman pleasure by saying a few constructive words. Sincere praise took little effort or time, but the effect was always positive and immediate. J.R.'s compliments had enabled her to hold her head a little higher. She caught him undressing her with his eyes and felt half-naked, but she didn't mind.

In that hour long taxi ride J.R. captured Patsy's interest with all types of subjects and she felt very relaxed with him.

"What do I have to do to get you to come out to dinner with me?" J.R. asked, as he helped Patsy with her luggage outside her apartment building in Shepherd's Bush.

"You would have to offer a candlelit dinner for two and a sip or two of white wine," she smiled.

J.R. beamed broadly, a glint in his eye.

"I can do better, how about a bottle or two of cold champagne?"

Patsy agreed, to J.R.'s delight. He told the taxi driver to wait and as he carried Patsy's suitcase up to the flat, the American looked up at the heavens gratefully. He was always thankful for whatever life offered him, but this was a bonus.

Leroy had fallen asleep in a pile on Patsy's sofa. He had made his way straight to her flat from the airport, but she wasn't there. He had let himself in with the spare keys he always carried and tripped over her suitcase behind the entrance door. It was unlike Patsy to arrive home from after a long, tiring flight and then go straight out again, but that's what it looked like. He tried calling her at her parents' place, but only got the answering machine. Then he called Patsy's best friend; if anyone knew where she was, Donna would. There was no answer there. He decided to go about his business. He still had to sort things out with the trainers and he had a stock check to do. There were one or two things waiting to be sorted out at the office also. What with one thing and another, (especially the latter), he didn't arrive back at Patsy's flat until midnight, by which time he had psyched himself up enough to excuse his lateness at the airport. He didn't need one immediately however, Patsy was still not there. He remembered how he had seen some chubby man with her in the taxi at the airport. A thought crossed his mind for a moment, but he discounted it. Weary from the chaotic day, he flopped exhausted, onto the comfortable Habitat sofabed and slipped quickly into a deep slumber — the dreams of which carried him half way across the world.

There he was, newly arrived in New York for the first time, it was a hot summer's day and people were traversing the streets in various forms of undress. But nobody batted an eyelid. The freakier the undress, the less people seemed to notice. For some reason however, people would roll around in laughter when he walked by. Leroy made his way all the way up Broadway, through Greenwich Village, mid-town, right up to 125th street. It was only when he got to the heart of Harlem that he noticed that he was having to look up at everybody. People seemed so much taller in New York. The buildings seemed considerably bigger than in England and everybody, even the women, seemed to dwarf him. Finally, he caught a glimpse of himself in a shop window and discovered for the first time that he was completely naked and only about two and a half feet tall, with a minuscule 'bully'...

He must have slept in the pitch darkness of the living room for hours and only awoke from his sleep at the sound of keys picking the front door lock. He heard low whispers and giggles. He could hear his woman's voice amongst it all in a state of gaiety. He didn't recognise the man's voice, but he stood up to await the newcomers' entrance.

The door swung open and Patsy — illuminated only by the light from the hallway — tumbled into the living room, followed by J.R. who was attempting to bite her ear, while Patsy fought him off half-heartedly, laughing playfully all the time. Leroy's nostrils flared up.

"What's going on?" he asked sternly.

Patsy and J.R. stopped, dead in their tracks. She flicked on the light switch and remained staring at Leroy with anger in her eyes. She sighed a sigh of frustration, then kissed her teeth.

"What's going on?" Leroy repeated. He felt uneasy but didn't want to show it.

J.R. gave Patsy a 'do you know this bum?' look. She sighed again.

"What the hell are you doing here?" Patsy asked.

Leroy couldn't believe his ears.

"Yeah what the hell *are* you doing here?" J.R. repeated after her.

"What the fuck are you talking about?!" Leroy's response served for both Patsy and J.R.'s questions.

Patsy turned to look at J.R., then at Leroy, then back to J.R. His eyes flicked from Leroy to Patsy then back to Leroy. Leroy simply waited. It was a stand-off.

"You better go," Patsy urged J.R.

The American gave her a quizzical look as if to say 'are you sure you want me to leave you alone with this lunatic'? Patsy insisted. The yank mumbled something before turning reluctantly towards the door.

"But you call me tomorrow," he told Patsy.

She nodded then closed the door behind him.

"First let's get something straight...!" Patsy began angrily, "this is my place... I can do what I want here... I can bring whoever I want here... remember that's the way *you* wanted it."

"Patsy, you've been gone for nearly two weeks... all I wanted was to spend some time alone with my woman... I've been calling all day, what happened?"

"What happened was that you weren't at the airport

40

to pick me up. I told you Leroy, I won't take this disrespect. If you can't be bothered to pick me up from the airport, there are plenty of guys around who can."

"Patsy, stop distressing me," Leroy said after a pause. Patsy was looking for a quarrel, but he wasn't really in the mood.

"When I point out something quite justifiably you say that I'm distressing you. No Leroy, I'm not distressing you... How long's it going to take you to understand that it's all about respect. You treat your friends with more respect than you do your woman. You wouldn't have let one of your friends down would you?"

"How d'you mean, Patsy?" Leroy sighed. "The amount of times I haven't been able to go out raving with my spars dem, or I've had to dig up early because you're flying back from somewhere... What about that?"

"Yeah, but at least you let them know when you're not showing up. You could have left a message at the airport for me to let me know you weren't coming."

Leroy sighed again. Irritated, Patsy kissed her teeth. She had seen that 'the woman just ah give me stress' look on his face too many times before. If he bothered trying to see it from her point of view he'd realise that it wasn't 'stress', she was simply vexed and with good reason. If he considered this stress, he should consider himself lucky that she hadn't yet shown him one tenth of the anger boiling up inside her.

"Honestly, you care so much about other people I wonder why you don't go off and have a relationship with one of your friends."

Leroy frowned. Enough was enough. As usual, his woman was making a meal of a morsel. Okay, he had missed her arrival, but why all the stress?

"Look Pat, I know I should have been there, but I had this deal going down — a big deal — I had a lot on my mind..."

'Yeah, right', Patsy thought. 'Big deal'. There was always a big deal going down and as far as Leroy was concerned, nothing was more important than the big deal. Who did he think he was?

"...Anyways, I'll make it up to you... Next time I'll drive you to the airport *and* I'll pick you up... Anything."

"Don't even try it," Patsy cut in with a warning finger.

It wasn't just about getting a lift from the airport, it was about doing things for each other generally. About showing how much you cared for one another. After three years, Leroy still couldn't find time to show how much he cared.

"I'm tired of having to fit into your plans, Leroy. What's the point of calling this a relationship? You never have time to make the little commitment that's required of you. I'm sick of it. If you love your wheelin' an' dealin' so much, if all your runnins are so important to you, go off and deal with them. But leave me alone, get out of my life. You're no good to me part-time."

At that moment, the phone went. Not the house phone, but Leroy's mobile. He reached into his breast pocket and flipped open the streamlined receiver deftly.

"Yowza! Yowza!" he called down the phone. "Bunny, ah you dat? I've been trying to get hold of you all day. So what you sayin', man?"

Leroy suddenly remembered something and covered the mouthpiece.

"Important call," he motioned to Patsy. "One minute."

He needn't have bothered with the promise. Patsy had already turned her back to him. The house phone was ringing. She had more important things to do with her time than to hang around waiting for 'Mr Mention' to finish his jugglings.

Was it too much to want a man who was loving and had a serious attitude towards his relationship, Patsy wondered. At 24-years-old, Patsy Hines had already decided that the dibbi-dibbi men she had previously gone out with would no longer feature in her life. She had explained that to Leroy from the very start. Theirs was going to be a partnership where each person contributed whatever was necessary to keep the love alive. Yet here she was three years down the line having to manners him about things he ought to know about. 'Treat your woman right' was at the top of every lover's list, why couldn't he understand that?

She picked up the house phone.

"Oh hi, J.R.... Yes, that's right..." she looked across at Leroy busy on his mobile and shook her head pitifully, "...My boyfriend. Remember that 'on-off' relationship I told you about, with this guy, well it's 'off' right now and I don't think he's going to be able to turn it back 'on'."

A look of deep concentration on Leroy's face, the mobile against his ear, Bunny's timely interruption had given him some breathing space. But his mind was only partly on the telephone conversation. He had to keep Bunny talking until he could think up a better excuse to get himself out of the situation. Patsy was right of course, he should have been there when he was supposed to be. When you know how your woman stays and how bad-minded she can be, you need to strive to keep a level vibe. She was always bound to see his not being there when she arrived, as the ultimate big diss.

Patsy listened to J.R. sweet-talking her down the line. He was calling her from a call box up the road from Patsy's flat to make sure that she was alright in the flat with "that madman". He offered to call the cops, but Patsy declined. She was going to deal with the situation and she didn't much care if Leroy heard her being less than complimentary about him down the line to J.R.

"Well he's not ideal so I'm keeping my options open..." Patsy said. "I prefer men who are hunks — tall and handsome, muscular — a little like you... and I like a man who's got one of those thin moustaches — exactly like you. And the sort of man that I like will have genuine prospects... I'm tired of hustlers..."

Patsy and J.R. continued to spar affably down the phone line. She had agreed to go to dinner with him earlier, not just out of anger with Leroy but because he was fun and because he was there to give her some time and consideration and a hug when she was feeling unappreciated. Nothing more than that. Leroy had taken their relationship for granted too many times for her to start feeling sorry for herself.

As innocent as the lunch was, there was no need to tell Leroy that she had taken a shower in J.R.'s Piccadilly hotel room. Leroy would have read more into it than it was, she had simply needed to freshen up before dinner. J.R. had insisted on her suggesting a really nice place to eat. As it was a warm day, they had settled for a popular floating restaurant moored on the Thames at the

Embankment. Throughout the meal, the American had been loud and very full of himself, but he was always charming, and yes, she couldn't deny it... she found him attractive and easy to talk to.

'Well,' she thought to herself, 'it's not unusual to sometimes feel you deserve better'. It was that simple, Patsy reflected. The best, the very best, was the absolute minimum requirement for any relationship. Not just a best friend or best lover, but the best treatment, the best vibes. She shouldn't have to settle for anything less. It had been different in the beginning when Leroy first dated her. She was just taking her finals at university. Leroy had been so sweet and had sent her a rose with the message: "You'll always be first class in my eyes." And it was fine for a year after that, but while he got more and more involved with making money, he became less of a best friend. She resented taking second place to all the business deals. And she hated his readiness to take a phone call in the middle of a serious discussion, as if whatever they had to discuss was always less important than the call.

Bunny continued talking down the phone. Leroy tried his best to concentrate. Bunny was Leroy's driver, responsible for distributing King Lee Enterprises' assorted products to the network of street sellers who worked for the business selling from makeshift unofficial pitches at crucial thoroughfares in the black community. Bunny eased his boss' worries and assured Leroy that he had been busy all day and that the training shoes were already on the open market.

How many times did he have to repeat himself, Leroy wondered. Patsy knew that everything he did was for their sake. Okay, he spent a lot of time doing deals and trying to make a dollar, but it was for her too. He had told her from the beginning that he was going to be rich. He didn't intend to struggle in life. He just needed Patsy to give him some space for a few years. He intended to make enough money to retire by the time he was 35. Everything was going smooth, according to plan. He just needed another five or six years and that one big break and he'd be done. Why couldn't Patsy just cool and accept that? He wasn't doing it just for himself, he was doing it for the two of them.

"...Well you know what they say," Patsy continued down the phone, "a good man is hard to find..."

She looked across the room at Leroy frowning at her. She didn't mind if he heard her, he needed to learn. He must have been joking when he thought that she would agree to be his baby mother at some stage, when all the evidence suggested that he would abandon her and she would have to deal with the job of raising 'Junior' alone.

"Well, if you know any good men, a really good man," Patsy continued mock-earnestly, "and he's available, give him my number... Friday is a possibility... you see Friday's my birthday and I've extended an invitation to a man with a habit of not showing up..."

She threw Leroy a piercing glance. He was still on his call and didn't notice.

"...I will, sure, if he doesn't show up, the invitation will be yours. Well call me on Friday evening and if I'm on my own I'll go out and celebrate my birthday with you."

She signed off with a "Ciao!" and replaced the

receiver. At the same time, Leroy snapped his mobile shut.

"I hope you haven't forgotten about Friday?" she said.

Friday? What was Friday? Leroy scanned his mind hurriedly. Of course, her birthday. He was spending the day with her.

"Don't worry yourself," he said with a big grin and a wink of his eye, "everything is safe for Friday."

"Yeah, like it was for the airport," Patsy countered unimpressed.

"Oh don't give me grief about that, Pat. I have apologised already."

Even as he pleaded, Leroy knew his woman well enough to know that she wouldn't let this one drop that easily. Even if she left it for now, it would come up again — raise its ugly head — maybe tomorrow, maybe next week, next month, next year; she would drag it up as it best suited her. If only there was a way of explaining that he had really been looking forward to spending the day with her. A man's intentions, however sincere, are not always the same as his actions. 'It could have happened to anybody', Leroy thought to himself. She was right, they hadn't spent much time with each other lately, but that was on account of all the business he had been doing. However, all work and no play makes Leroy a dull boy.

Patsy had tired of Leroy's excuses. Today he had come within an inch of wrecking their relationship, but he didn't seem to realise it. That was his problem, she decided with a shrug of the shoulders, then disappeared into the bathroom to run a hot bubble bath.

"So on Friday we're going to spend the day having a

picnic together at Kew Gardens and then go out for dinner in the evening," she called out through the half-open bathroom door. She didn't want any mistakes, because she didn't want any more excuses. She had let Leroy off tonight. By rights, she had previously vowed not to continue the relationship if he dissed her again, but when push came to shove she was willing to allow him one final chance. "The arrangements are in your hands, you're taking care of everything."

"Don't you hear me already, Patsy? I said, 'yeah'. Everything's under control. Alright?"

'It shouldn't have to be this way', Patsy thought. Leroy ought to use his initiative and surprise her. But she couldn't afford to leave anything to chance. She was determined to celebrate her birthday. If Leroy also thought it important, everything would go smoothly. If he didn't, she was better off without him.

'It shouldn't have to be this way', Leroy told himself. He had stuck by her throughout their relationship and tried to do the right thing. She had said in the beginning that she wanted a man with ambition, where else was she going to find someone with as much ambition as he had? Honestly, sometimes he got the feeling that she was jealous of his success. He pulled out the wad of notes from his leather money belt and flicked through the roll. He smiled to himself — cash really was king.

CHAPTER 4

Leroy's various business deals left him little time to attend to his woman's needs and desires, yet he managed to make time for the Westview Youth Project. The Project was vital to his plans to become wealthy and successful. It had given him status and through it he had become a respectable member of the black middle classes. He now counted policemen, clergy, MPs and judges amongst his friends. All the 'get rich quick' books encourage their students to befriend powerbrokers, and Leroy had a feeling that his contacts would soon come in useful.

The Westview Estate in Harlesden was a throwback to earlier 'pack 'em in thick and tight' housing policies. Its buildings were dominated by high-level outdoor walkways and distinguished by the rubber-matted corridors within and by the chilly winds which blew around the high-rise blocks at the centre of the Estate. The many millions of pounds that had been poured into Westview over the years could not disguise the fact that it was an eyesore. Despite the well-lit landscaped gardens, security systems and dotted murals of Bob Marley, Marcus Garvey and diverse other 'black heroes in the hall of fame', the Estate still had the reputation

49

for being grim, a bleak and brutal 'ghetto' into which local authorities herded large numbers of the black community in the sixties, seventies and eighties, resulting simultaneously in requests by nearly the entire body of the Estate's early white residents for transfers to housing anywhere else but Westview... The flats inside however, were spacious and comfortable and many residents had happily lived there for years without complaint.

The Westview Youth Project was at the heart of the Estate, both figuratively and literally. The youth club-cum-community centre was a standing testament to the tenacity and durability of the black youth who had fought to establish it and had continued the struggle to keep it open and alive. The large numbers of Asian, African and 'Black British' residents who had always stood firm alongside the Caribbean youth of the Project, also considered the Centre as their 'victory'.

As Leroy's easily distinguishable BMW pulled into the car space outside the Centre, a few of the youths hanging around outside the club hailed him up.

"My yout'," Leroy said, touching fists with one of them as he climbed out of the car.

To one side of the Centre was a makeshift basketball court with a couple of hoops, where two teenagers — both stripped to the waist in the early evening sun and sweating profusely — were engaged in a game of one-on-one.

"Yaow Chinna!" Leroy called over to the taller of the two six footers. "You ready to try for some pocket money?"

The youth smiled at him and nodded.

"Then mek me see the shot, man."

Leroy walked over to the youths. The taller youth, no more than thirteen or fourteen years of age, took his place in the middle of the basketball court. He steadied himself, concentrated, with his eyes fixed on the hoop at one end of the court. With the basket ball balanced delicately in his hands, he took aim and took an accurate shot at the hoop. The ball went in cleanly.

"Wicked shot!" Leroy congratulated the boy. "Two more baskets and my man's gonna be £20 richer."

Chinna steadied himself for the second shot. By now, the small group of youths standing outside the Centre had wandered over to see what was going down. Chinna kept his concentration on the basket in front of him. He bounced the ball once, twice, three times... his mind locked onto the mission at hand. He finally released the ball, less accurately this time and it balanced precariously on top of the hoop before squeezing it's way through with a clatter. There was a tremendous cheer from his assembled colleagues.

Leroy teased Chinna some by reaching in his pocket for his wad and pulling out a £20 note and shouting manically at him from under the hoop, waving his hands frantically to distract the youth.

"Come on now 'Magic', show us what you can do, man. One more shot for the big jackpot."

"You're just trying to put him off, Leroy, it's not fair," said the youth who had been playing with Chinna earlier.

"Who said anything about fair?" Leroy retorted. "We're talking basketball, man. You think the Rockets beat the Knicks because they were *fair*? We're talking winning, man. If my man's going over Stateside to make it in the NBA, he's gotta be a winner."

"It's no problem," said Chinna, calmly steadying himself for the throw.

Leroy continued distracting him from below the hoop, shouting and gesticulating. Chinna concentrated hard. His friends were drawn in closer, in anxious anticipation. They held their breath. One more bounce and finally Chinna released the ball...

West London plays the best basketball in the UK, that was an indisputable fact in the opinion of the youths of Westview. These kids had turned basketball into an art form and the Estate's residents often gathered for hours just watching them playing their amazing shots. There were kids who lived on and around the Estate who played such good basketball that they would have got scholarships to the top universities of their choice if they were living in the States. Chinna was such a youth. He not only had the inborn talent for the game but he was also strong, fast, disciplined... and it looked like he was going to grow another ten inches, at least, the rate he was going. Chinna had all the qualities to go to the very top of the basketball profession and come out a millionaire, but unfortunately for him he lived in England where the national sport of black America was ignored because it's "not exactly cricket." But Leroy had big plans for Chinna. The youngster played some breathtaking basketball and through a friend of his on Channel 4's basketball programme, Leroy had got wind of an American college basketball scout who was coming to England shortly. Chinna had to get his free throws into shape if he was going to get a look in and if he did get a look in, Leroy intended to manage him.

...The ball sailed into the air loftily; it seemed to hang suspended forever. Then suddenly it dipped a little too soon. The ball crashed into the ring with an echoing shudder, accompanied by the collective groan of despondency from young Chinna's clutch of supporters.

Jovially, Leroy plucked up the ball on the rebound and shuffled it between his legs before lifting himself high up and raising the ball above the hoop for an easy slam dunk. Then in a sports announcer voice he teased:

"And Leroy Massop, the centre from the Chicago Bulls, the man they brought in after the irreplaceable Michael Jordan suddenly retired, wins the NBA championship for his team for the tenth year in succession!"

Leroy lifted his arms up in mock victory. The youngsters gathered around began to drift away as the older man started showing off.

"Well, I nearly made it this time, y'know," Chinna warned, "so next time you just make sure you bring that money with you, 'cause I'll be needing it."

"Sure, sure," Leroy chided, "*nearly* ain't good enough, yout'man. Keep practising is what I'm telling you, practice. Three in a row, that's all you've got to throw and the prize is yours."

He bodypunched the youths playfully a couple of times then made his way into the Centre.

Leroy Massop had started working voluntarily with the fledgling Westview Youth Project, when it opened a couple of years before, following many months of tension between the local youths and the police. The residents had demanded the Centre to remedy the lack of social facilities for black youth on the Estate and to provide an alternative to the perpetual nothingness of life in the area. The council had finally agreed. The two-storey building, a former primary school on the Estate, was finally funded as a way of easing the threat of insurrection. At the head of the Resident's Association was a regular thorn in the side of the authorities — the local pentecostal pastor, Rev. Francis Marshall, an influential and enterprising young militant priest, with a fancy for expensive silk shirts, Gucci loafers, jeri curls and large gold medallions.

With Leroy's contacts at the local council, the Centre eventually got funding. Then successful businessman Elroy Bailey got involved. He had once attempted to launch the first black bank in the UK, but the established banks had gone to extraordinary lengths to make sure that there was no way the black community's annual £10 billion was going to end up in a black bank. Before long, with Bailey's fundraising help, the Youth Project was also serving meals daily to the local pensioners. It had now grown to include a child day care centre, music and cultural events, and a series of co-operative businesses including a laundrette, a hairdressers and workshops for things like sewing and photography and a well-equipped pre-production studio down in the basement. Today the Project was not just a place for recreation and services to the community, but also the most successful 'black business' in the area.

As far as Leroy was concerned, British post-war immigration policy of 'assimilation' was a joke. Britain never intended for the immigrants who came into the country in large numbers to clean up after the war, to stay permanently. Otherwise they would have made adequate provisions — cultural and otherwise — for the second generation, the children of the immigrants... but they never did. Education remained therefore, culturally biased in the secret hope that the immigrants would accept that they had outstayed their welcome and eventually return to Jamaica, Barbados, Nigeria, Ghana and the other countries in the so-called 'commonwealth'. No matter what was said officially, the British governments of the fifties and sixties were simply not down with guessing who was coming to dinner. The kids on the Westview Estate faced the same old racism in school where they were confronted by teachers with the same old stereotype of the black 'underachiever'. Their parents still talked about them becoming lawyers and doctors and so on — not an unreasonable ambition from parents who knew their children's worth. The brightest of these kids were capable of distinguishing themselves in their A-Levels and going on to university. However, they were cast in classes where their education would serve them only in the most menial tasks. It took a long time for these youngsters to recover from their school experiences. It changed their lives permanently.

Increasing numbers of youths who did not belong on the Estate had also started using the Project as it was the only reasonable place to go to of an evening, and because of the cheap Caribbean food available. The longer they spent at the Centre, the more they would vent their feelings about the education which had thrown them on the scrap heap. Often they would turn their anger and resentment into something positive and take up one of the many vocational classes available at the Centre. The police had recently claimed the praise for the reduction in crime on the Estate, but these youths knew it had nothing to do with the cops.

The meeting was already in progress when Leroy stepped into the Centre's main hall. Assembled in a semi-circle in the middle of the hall, was a multi-million dollar 'think-tank' team of West London's black dignitaries. The dozen or so men and women gathered were the steering committee, selected from the very best pedigree. As well as Elroy Bailey and Frank Marshall, there was television news presenter Marva Grant, Yvette Mampie — the first black woman MP — and Lyndon Douglas who ran a successful employment agency which specialised in getting good jobs for black youth. Also present was the local community policeman. Leroy hoped that that didn't mean trouble.

"Oh Mr. Massop, so glad you could make it," Rev. Marshall called out with overstated irony as Leroy stepped in. "Now we can start the meeting properly. First let me welcome back Sergeant Taylor, who you all know already. He will be speaking on both of the points on the agenda. First of all, we have been asked by the DTI once again for information leading to the arrest of pirate broadcasters they believe are sending signals from a location in this area. Sergeant Taylor, you would like to say a few words on this?"

The policeman, a pink-faced, chubby man with a self-important cockney accent — one of the few officers who could walk about on the Estate without it resulting in a full-scale red alert amongst the local youths — stood up and addressed the meeting.

56

"Yes, as Reverend Marshall said, any information you can give us about the youngsters who are sending these illegal broadcasts would be greatly appreciated by the DTI and ourselves. We believe that it's coming from somewhere on this Estate. I would like to remind you that not only is it an offence to broadcast without a radio licence but it is also highly dangerous. These pirates are endangering the communication of airlines flying overhead on their way to Heathrow Airport. Just think how terrible it would be if a planeload of tourists crashed on the Westview Estate, just because of some pirate radio station broadcasting illegally!"

"Oh honestly Sergeant, you're talking a load of crap," said the aggressive Yvette Mampie. She could be a difficult woman and demanding — as the entire House of Commons knew — but her influence was immense so she was always taken seriously. "The Met must really be cutting down on the police force if you have to ask for our help in catching a bunch of kids. Honestly!"

Rev. Marshall apologised to the officer on Mampie's behalf.

"Please Yvette, let us show some respect to the Sergeant..."

Rev Francis Marshall prided himself on understanding youth, talking their language and understanding where they were coming from, because like the biggest raggamuffin or rudie out there, he had been a roughneck in his teenage years. At 15, he became disillusioned with his family's clean-living, church-going habits and rebelled by going out drinking and dancing in clubs, but within a year he returned to the church. So he understood the spiritual needs of rebellious youth, but he refused to accept any 'slackness' from them, especially when it came to music. Rev. Marshall was not a lone voice in the battle against reggae music with explicit sexual references and gun lyrics; he had a whole congregation behind him campaigning to 'Smash The Slackness'. His pentecostal church saw slackness as a major battle in the war for the souls of the young, in the struggle between Saturday night and Sunday morning. Rev. Marshall felt that musical talent should be used not to promote promiscuity but to inspire people spiritually. Towards this end, he had formed the Westview Community Gospel Choir, which was the hippest, trendiest, funkiest gospel choir on this side of the ocean. Several top pop stars had already used the Choir to enhance their songs and the latest news was that it had even got its own record deal. However funky it was and even though it recruited a number of youngsters from the area, the Choir was seen by the majority as still a gospel choir and that was definitely not 'dope'. Needless to say, other less spiritual battles took place at the Centre, youth against youth.

"Perhaps we could get onto the next topic..." Rev. Marshall continued. Now all of you know that we were hoping to get a notable figure to officially open the Centre on Friday... Well good news: after six months of secret negotiations with Buckingham Palace..."

A hush fell around the room, as each member of the committee waited with baited breath.

"...Princess Diana, the Princess of Wales, has agreed to come..."

There was a resounding cheer around the room. None

of them had expected news this good.

The young pastor continued:

"Because of the tight security surrounding such events I was unable to say anything to any of you before... Perhaps you would like to fill us in on the details concerning this matter Sergeant?"

The officer stood up again.

"Yes, thank you Reverend. Now of course with a royal visit, security will be extremely tight... Only a few selected members of the Centre's youngsters will be able to meet her. Everybody in this room will get to meet the Princess personally and the Reverend has kindly selected members of the Westview Community Gospel Choir, who he believes are an admirable representation of the youth from the Centre — to meet her Royal Highness. The outstanding, upright kids of the Choir will then put on a little mini-performance for the Princess. Apart from that I'm afraid, the Centre will be off limits to everybody else... for security reasons..."

Leroy spoke up at this point.

"As Youth Development Officer for the Project, I'm not happy about that. This Centre's about the local youths. You can't just ask them not to be around because a royal is visiting. If you're gonna be giving the Princess a gospel performance, the other kids should be allowed to give her a performance of their music."

Sergeant Taylor reiterated that for 'security reasons' the Princess could not meet all of the youths.

"We're lucky to get the Princess coming to visit," he insisted. "If the Special Branch thought she was going to be surrounded by local youth, they would probably call it off."

Leroy hadn't intended to open a can of worms and spark off a lively debate amongst the steering committee, but that's what he had done. Leroy and his main ally Lyndon, insisted that they could smell a rat. This was another attempt to divide and rule — those 'model' youths who wore starched, white shirts and blouses and had their hair in conservative haircuts would get to meet the Princess, while youths wearing kangols, baggy jeans and carrying ten pounds of 'cargo' would be treated as lepers. Rev. Marshall countered that it was a question of selecting the best behaved youth to meet the Princess and yeah, the Choir did seem to be synonymous with good behaviour. He wanted the Princess to meet the best of black British youth not the 'roughneck crew.' He couldn't believe that Leroy was serious when suggesting that they should entertain the Princess with 'street' music.

"This isn't just an issue about the Westview Youth Project..." the Reverend began in his oratorical way, as if speaking from the pulpit. "The Princess agreeing to visit us is an honour. Make no mistake my brothers and sisters, the eyes of Britain will be upon us and how the Princess is treated here will be seen as representative of the whole black community up and down the country. You cannot seriously expect me to agree to their performing ragga music for the Princess... or what are they calling it nowadays, 'jungle', can you believe it...?" he appealed to his fellow committee members. "We can't invite them to come and run the place red, remember they actually call it jungle... as if we were uncivilised... No there's enough illegal pirate stations playing 'jungle' music without us having to present it to the Princess

60

also."

The Reverend had heard the latest music craze and concluded that like ragga, it was about the woman's body. The girls danced in their bikini outfits showing more of their bodies than good taste would allow and jiggling it for everybody to see.

Leroy frowned, Marshall was always blaming all the negative things on the radical youths. He claimed to understand them, but when you really checked it, the Reverend equated 'badness' with the way a youth dressed. He blamed the local 'ragga' youths for every crime. Leroy knew the youths better and knew that they could be cool and they could be destructive, but also that they didn't skylark and were no different from any of the 'decent' youths in the church. Hearing the Reverend speak, Leroy could understand the hostility felt by young, black militants for the elders of the community whose survival tactics — for themselves and their loved ones — appeared like the antics of 'Uncle Toms' marinated in cowardice.

By the end of the meeting, the more establishment-friendly members agreed to co-operate with the police and to only allow the gospel choir and a pair of heavily-vetted model young achievers to meet the royal guest.

The meeting went on into late in the evening when those in attendance finally emerged from the Centre, climbed into their vehicles and drove off in their different directions. By this time, only Chinna remained in the courtyard outside, practising free throws into the hoop. But otherwise the area seemed deserted, Chinna's friend having made his way over to the Hammersmith side of things where they were hoping to bumrush the first UK appearance by a certain top ragga artist from Jamaica. Tickets had sold out weeks before, but Chinna was determined to make it in by any means necessary.

Lyndon said that he would stay behind with Leroy to lock up the Centre. The two friends stood watching Reverend Marshall's car drive out of the Estate. They both looked at each other and gave a sigh of relief.

"Bwoy, I thought that meeting would never end," said Lyndon.

Leroy glanced at his watch.

"We should have been on the air an hour ago," he said.

Lyndon stuck two fingers in his mouth and blew a shrill whistle that echoed amongst the surrounding blocks of flats. Within minutes, youthful silhouettes appeared stealthily from different directions, carrying record and tape decks and stacks of 12 inch records.

It didn't take long to set up the popular Groove FM in the attic space under the roof of the Centre. The space had been empty for years after the school had closed down and now rarely did anybody in the Youth Project committee bother to check what was going on up there. Leroy had cleared the attic with the help of Lyndon, Johnny Ringo and a few other youths. They had now managed to turn it into a comfortable, if spartan, radio studio. The station's engineers and deejays were adept and experienced enough in their work to be able to set up the equipment in no time at all.

At only seventeen, Johnny Ringo was easily the most popular radio deejay in the whole of West London. It was rumoured that the high level of truancy at comprehensive schools from Holland Park to Wembley was due to Ringo's late, late Wednesday night supermixes.

Eventually the station went on air. Johnny Ringo took the mike and first apologised "to the massive and crew and god knows who..." for Groove coming on air an hour late, "...due to certain 'technical' difficulties." But there was no time for "chatting and backbiting" and without further ado he dropped the needle on the latest 'junglist' anthem, 'Wicked an' Wicked an' Wicked an' Wild', with its ear-shattering speeded up drum beat, punctuated by a sample from a recent Buju Banton hit.

To Leroy, it all sounded like chaos and total confusion, but he was a businessman who couldn't deny that 'jungle' had immense commercial potential and when it went overground and busted into the charts, he intended to be in the right place at the right time. That's why he had set up Groove FM with his homeboy Lyndon. They didn't see it as illegal. It was time the community started turning its back on culturally-biased British laws. The laws for radio stations as they stood were made to exclude the black youth who were in the first place singularly responsible for the government being forced to relax the laws to allow some incremental stations. As far as Lyndon and Leroy were concerned, Groove FM was a community station. The only thing that Groove didn't possess was a legal licence and that made it 'illegal'. It had better programmes and deejays and played a better selection of music than most other stations, as was testified by the number of listeners who regularly supported the station. Groove FM spoke for the youth of the neighbourhood. But the way the government and the police saw it, they were breaking the law. There had to be a way of getting one of the legal licences being offered by the Department of Trade and Industry in their latest round of frequency sellouts, but Leroy couldn't see it. If they had a proper licence, they could start attracting advertisers and earning some real corn. Everybody was going to get paid properly; the youths trusted him and he wasn't going to let them down. But if they didn't get a legal licence, they would have to continue sneaking into the Centre in the evening and broadcasting as a pirate for as long as it took.

Apart from Lyndon, the other committee members would never have approved of the station, especially Rev. Marshall who would have called on the wrath of the Lord to chastise these lawbreakers, before calling the police and informing on the youngsters' law-breaking. Like Leroy, Lyndon, given the chance, was an intelligent hustler, so he quickly came in on the deal. The neighbourhood kids possessed untapped abilities... As long as the youths got paid for their talents it was fair enough that he and his partner also got some change out of it.

"I've just had a wicked idea!" Leroy shouted enthusiastically as they watched the young radio deejay deliver his lyrics fast and efficiently down the microphone. "If we could go legal, we'd be the ruffest station out there, right?"

Lyndon agreed. No other station could test Groove when it came to music. All they needed was that licence and it would all be legal.

"Supposing we could get the Princess of Wales to sponsor us...?"

Lyndon thought about it.

"It's a crazy idea," he said. "So crazy it might just work... But how are you going to do that?"

"I've got a plan," Leroy began. "When she comes on Friday..."

He told Lyndon his idea. It was a long shot, but it was worth a try. With the Princess backing them, the DTI would have to give them a radio licence.

It was a warm evening, so Leroy drove home with his top down, the radio tuned to the sounds of Groove FM. He ran over the plan in his head again. When the Princess came on Friday... Friday... Shit! He had forgotten Friday was Patsy's birthday and he was already under manners. What was he going to do? He felt his leather money belt for his wad of banknotes and pulled it out reassuringly. When you have 'nuff cash available, you can get anything you want.

CHAPTER 5

Patsy sat up in her double-size water bed, the black silk sheet pulled up to her chest, reading a copy of the Jamaica Enquirer — which she had picked up when her plane touched down in Kingston:

A Kingstonian known as 'Badness' recently picked up two chops in the back, at the hands of a country man in Anchovy, St James, Montego Bay.

'Badness' who is a notorious gunman was living with his baby mother, alias 'Agony' in Kingston, but they couldn't agree so she left with her 9-month old baby to live with relatives in the country.

'Badness' missed his 'Agony' so much that he went to Montego Bay on a regular basis to visit her. As neighbours put it:

"He always got 'nuff respect from relatives aware of his notoriety as a robber and gun-hawk from Kingston."

One neighbour was quoted as saying: "Everybody inna fe de house 'fraid fe him. If him seh 'run', yuh bettah run. If him seh 'jump' yuh bettah jump high. Him went like King Kong inna de place."

One day he went to visit Agony but was told by relatives

that she'd packed her things and "gone live over de breddah yard."

Badness rushed to the said house with blood "inna him eye", and confronted the boyfriend who was on the verandah in his underpants:

"Yuh see me yah, me nuh want see my yout' wid step-fadda, seen? So me come fe mash up de house."

Badness then turned to his baby mother and asked:

"Ah dem yah life yuh want live wid my yout'?"

After some slaps to her face he ordered her to collect her things and follow him. Trembling with fear she obeyed.

By this time the scandal had spread throughout the neighbourhood and the sizeable crowd which had now gathered roared with laughter at the sight of the boyfriend standing helplessly on the verandah, still in his underpants.

Agony was left at her relatives' house while Badness went back to town, but by the following morning she was back at her boyfriend's house. Badness returned a few days later, only to be told: "Agony gone back ah de breddah yard."

Like a real Kingston bad man, Badness headed back to the house with the crowd behind him.

He reached the front door and kicked it open, brandishing a ratchet knife.

The boyfriend, seeing the crowd at his gate again, resolved not to be humiliated a second time. He reached for his cutlass and pursued the unsuspecting Badness, eventually giving him two chops on the back.

As the first blows struck, Badness immediately dropped his ratchet knife and ran down the hill bawling, "Murder! Murder! Help!"

The boyfriend ran after, but was only able to 'capture' a shoe that the Kingstonian bad bwoy had lost in his haste.

Badness has not been seen in the area since.

Patsy giggled uncontrollably. The Enquirer always had good stories. In bed beside her, Leroy woke up feeling randy, the romantic Chanel scent on the sheets never failed to have that effect. But then Winnie Mandela cooled his desires as she usually did, staring down at him from a poster on the wall opposite, with a disconcerting expression on her face and raising her right hand in an uncompromising clenched fist salute. Leroy closed his eyes for a moment and tried to cast Winnie out of his mind. He turned his head, and slid a warm hand under the sheet, slowly caressing Patsy's breasts.

"So what's so funny?" he asked, wiping the sleep from his eyes.

"I brought a copy of the Enquirer with me. There's a good story on the front page, you should read it."

She handed Leroy the paper, still giggling. Leroy read the story quickly.

"It's not that funny," he concluded.

"That story should be a lesson to all you black men who keep forgetting that they leave their women at home with love in their eyes and lust in their hearts. That's a dangerous situation. Remember, for every yearning woman sitting at home, there are a dozen handymen only too ready to be of service to them."

Leroy sat up puzzled. He was sure that Patsy was referring to their relationship. If she had intended to make him think of the suave American, she had succeeded. Maybe 'fatty' had called her, Leroy wasn't sure and he didn't want to ask her straight out either.

One thing was clear, there was no way he was going to let some yank tender to his lawn while he was out making dollars.

Leroy Massop knew when he met his woman that she wouldn't do things like cook for him. She had more important things to do with her time. She was a middle class woman and middle class women simply didn't cook for their men, she insisted. She told him that carrying devotion so far had gone out of fashion with women. And she was a new type of woman who intended to live her life to the max fulfiling her ambitions, not slaving over a hot stove for any man. As he recalled it, it was Patsy's idea also that they should each keep their separate flats after they started going out, even though she was now claiming that it was his idea. The arrangement suited Leroy fine; they both wanted to maintain their independence in the relationship. They both agreed that not living on top of each other had kept their love alive. And even though Leroy couldn't say how long their relationship would last, to him it felt like it would last forever, especially when he realised that calling her 'sweetness' once in a while made her look like she had heaven in her eyes. And even though he had plenty of opportunity to have other women around his flat for a night, Leroy wasn't really interested. Everybody kept telling him, in Patsy he had a woman that men would kill for. A nice, intelligent, educated, conscious girl from a good family and well-spoken. Now Leroy knew that all the money in the world couldn't buy a woman like that. He simply wanted to earn all the money in the world so that he could spend it on his woman, shower her with it...

That's how much he loved her.

All that wasn't enough for Patsy. She sat at the breakfast table in her spacious, fully-fitted, modern kitchen — with its black and white tiled floors and huge south-facing windows through which the early morning summer sun always blazed — going through snapshots from her stay in Barbados with the rest of the airline crew. Photos of her sunbathing by the hotel pool and others of her looking out across the ocean. It was only a few days, but they were happy days for her. Yet, she would have preferred it if she and Leroy had travelled there together on holiday. She would much rather have spent her time in Barbados with the man she loved than with a British Airways flight crew.

Leroy had let himself into her flat late the night before in really good spirits, and had woken her gently in the morning with soft kisses. He had treated her like she wished he would treat her always, and when it came to making love, well, she had almost forgotten that it could be so sweet; Leroy deserved a standing ovation, he had been so giving, like he used to be before he started timing their moments together. She wanted it to be like this always, why couldn't Leroy understand that? It cost so little to make the effort of turning every day into a romantic day. Leroy really had the power to do that when he wanted to, but sadly those moments were becoming rarer and rarer.

Who could say why love had brought them to the point they were at, and where it would eventually lead? All Patsy knew was that she loved this guy. Despite all his faults and the fact that their relationship never seemed high on his list of priorities, she couldn't imagine a future without him being part of her life in some way or other. They had something special together for which there was no substitute.

Leroy wasn't just her lover, he was much more, he was her brother, her best friend. Whenever she flew off with her job she was always saving experiences to tell Leroy about when she got home. She wished that they were going off around the world together, sharing those experiences, but Leroy had said that he wasn't ready. He wasn't ready to get married and he wasn't ready to live with her. She had been ready for a long while, but because he was so negative Patsy said she wasn't ready either: she wasn't ready to live together and she wasn't ready to have kids — definitely not, and when she was, she intended only to have kids if Leroy was ready to make his contribution. She didn't fancy bringing up a kid on her own.

Leroy stepped out of the shower with a towel around his waist and wandered through Patsy's open-plan living room — decorated with all its African ornaments – into the kitchen.

"So, did you miss me when you were away?" he asked.

"Don't flatter yourself," Patsy teased.

"Not even my good loving?" he smiled.

"If you're talking about last night, I thought it was you screaming on and on about how good my loving was, remember? It sounded like you missed me?"

"Whatd'ya mean, man? Of course I missed you, Pat. Every hour of the day..."

"Oh yeah?" she said cynically, "you found time to think about me in-between all those big deals, did you?"

71

They were always sparring like this. It was an unspoken mutual challenge — whoever had the last word was the winner.

"So are you looking forward to your birthday tomorrow?" Leroy asked.

"Don't tell me, you're about to say that you can't make it?"

"Take it easy, Pat. I'm not going to say that, don't be so suspicious. I'm just asking if you're looking forward to it."

"Yes," she said after a pause, "I'll only become twenty-five once so I'm looking forward to spending just one day with you, far from the hustle and bustle of our hectic lives and miles away from friends, family and any other interruptions. That'll be fun for a change."

Leroy had decided that he should also spend today with Patsy. He had lifted the phone off the hook to eliminate all interruptions so that they could really be alone together for a change. It was a way of safeguarding himself for not being with Patsy the whole day tomorrow, for he had already decided that he had to be at the Centre when the Princess came the next day. Leroy considered coming clean and breaking it to his woman gently, or maybe he should just give it to her straight and stand back at a reasonable distance, waiting for any unexpected move, ready to counter it? That was just too dangerous. He had to avoid getting her in a real vexation. There was no way he could tell his woman that he would be late because he was attending a reception for the Princess of Wales. Patsy would flip, take it as the ultimate diss that he was standing her up for another woman!

At least they would now spend a whole day together *before* her birthday and that added up to pretty much the same thing. They didn't have to meet up just on the day did they? It would be great to spend the whole day together, but then he would lose his one chance to meet someone like the Princess face-to-face, someone who was a real power player and who could be useful as a contact in the future, someone who could help the radio station. He knew that Patsy would lose her temper and be upset, but if she realised that they were able to get a legal pirate station out of it, she would understand, he was sure of it. Especially after he eased her down on her living room rug to tease her up and hug her up and squeeze her up, and pepper her with the most delicate kisses and the most tender caresses after which he would give her a good rub up. The situation would definitely get tense for a while if he didn't show up, but once she had read all the love letters he was going to write, after he had given her the full one hundred percent niceness with his body lying next to hers, she would forgive him. She always did, because he had that golden touch. It would take a while, but she would understand eventually.

"So how much did you miss me, then?" Patsy teased poking Leroy in the ribs.

"How much? Precisely how much?"

"Precisely."

"Let me count the ways: I missed you to the breadth and height and depth of my soul."

Patsy smiled and punched him in the stomach playfully.

"Now you're making fun of me."

She stood up and made her way to the shower. 'When Leroy tries, he can even be poetic,' she thought pleasingly. She had to get him to try a lot more. She wasn't prepared to forget that he had kept her waiting, but while Leroy was still able to make her laugh and make her happy, their relationship was the most important thing in her life.

Leroy listened to his woman showering in the bathroom. He really had missed her. She wasn't just his partner, he saw her as his 'baby' and he wanted to take care of her. He couldn't think of many things he wouldn't do for her. But she shouldn't make him promise things that he couldn't fulfil. There was enough 'obligation' in a relationship without distressing it some more. It wasn't his fault that the Princess' visit was falling on the same day as Patsy's birthday, was it? For Patsy, romance was about the little things, for him life was about the big things. She was more into the small gestures that made life together special and less into extravagant, expensive gestures. She came from a middle-class background anyway and Leroy had concluded that that was why she didn't have the same passion for making a lot of money that he had. He wanted to use every opportunity and make each and every moment count like time was running out, while she looked forward to him performing the little surprises like candle-lit dinners, weekend getaways together and that sort of thing. And Leroy had tried. Patsy said that he didn't devote time to the relationship, but look at all the things he had done... He had memorised all their anniversaries — the day they first met, their first date, the first time they made love, the first time he said, "I love you..." He had a standing order with the local florist who he had given a list with all the basic dates plus a few 'just because' dates. Now Patsy couldn't say she hadn't had any flowers. And he was always sending her some kind of greetings card to tell her how much he loved her — funny cards, romantic cards, sexy cards and different home-made cards. And when she returned home from her air stewardess job, he always made time to see her and would often stay in for dinner by candlelight after which they'd make their own popcorn before watching a romantic movie on the video. Later he would surprise her with a midnight massage. And every now and then he took pleasure in doing those little romantic things he knew she loved, like buying her a bottle of Dom Perignon, as a 'thank you' for doing the shopping, or tying a ribbon around her morning cup of coffee. Once he even hired a violinist to play for them over dinner at Patsy's flat. There wasn't a thing he wouldn't do for her, after all this was his woman, the woman he wanted to grow old with. "The best is yet to come," he often assured her.

He loved her, there was no doubt about it, but Patsy had to understand that he had to spend a lot of time making money. He had seen his father slave in two jobs to build a home for his family and he had watched helplessly as his father lost the little he had acquired in life trying to speculate in property. Leroy had vowed that he would one day restore his father's pride, every penny his father had lost. Above all else, Leroy had to make sure that the same thing didn't happen to him, on the contrary he had to be as rich as possible and as fast as possible so that he could still enjoy the fruits of his labour while he was young. That was why he was so fascinated by the lives of the rich and famous which he read about in American magazines such as Black Wealth, Black Enterprise and Black Millionaires which are crammed from cover to cover with 'rags to riches' stories. Leroy wanted to be rich. He was comfortable already, but he knew that he was blessed with talents that could make his wealth even greater. And he wasn't going to stop using those talents until he was seriously loaded. He had already decided several times over how he was going to spend his first million.

Patsy didn't see it that way at all. She had told him last night when they got back, exactly what she thought.

"I have to listen to you and you also ought to listen, with your ears, mind and heart, to what I say. Listen for the meaning behind my words, and the meaning behind my actions. You sometimes work overtime with your business, right? Why not occasionally work overtime on our relationship? Take a rest from making money. Money can't buy you love, you know."

Patsy stepped out of the shower and dried herself slowly. To her surprise, Leroy had prepared a tremendous breakfast for her. He had spread a white tablecloth on her round oak coffee table with the carved legs in the living room, in the centre of which was her ornamental carved African gourd filled with peanuts, lemons and limes. Beside it was, freshly squeezed tangerine juice in chilled champagne glasses, then a plate of scrambled eggs, sliced red onions marinated in lemon juice and pickapeppa sauce, fried green tomatoes and a pot of freshly ground bustelo coffee. She looked up to her man, beaming with pride. He was beautiful, and yet, somehow disillusionment had started seeping into her mind. She was just *so* weary of straining herself in this relationship.

She smiled and sat down to eat, happy because she had forgiven Leroy instead of throwing him out.

CHAPTER 6

Sergeant Taylor waited for a break in the fast moving midday traffic before crossing the busy road in front of the Estate to the crowd of youths hanging on the other side, their gold chains, bracelets, chopperettas, rings (and even gold teeth!) glistening in the afternoon sun. Posing like bad bwoys on the corner, the youths observed the comings and goings of the many police officers with suspicion. Too many innocent youths had been arrested and harassed too many times for them to feel comfortable about the heavy police presence in their area or for it to go unnoticed. Instinct told them that this was yet another example of "babylon trying to harass da youts." They all recognised Taylor however, and weren't surprised when he came over and started chatting and joking with them.

Taylor got on well with most of the local youths, but he knew that he was only tolerated as long as he didn't try to make any arrests, otherwise their thin veneer of tolerance would quickly disappear and he would find himself surrounded.

Dressed, as was the fashion amongst the youth, in casual, loose-fitting clothes and designer label sportswear, the youngsters looked relaxed, comfortable and cool compared to the officers in their tight blue uniforms. The taste for expensive brand name clothes was endemic amongst the youth as testified by designer names like Karl Kani emblazoned across their baggy T-shirts. Just like their predecessors, the rudies of old who stood on the very same street corners, these youngsters had nothing more promising vocationally than some kind of casual work to look forward to. They were quietly angry about conditions in the UK which had hardly improved for them or their parents before them over the years. Many of them had already decided that they weren't taking shit from anybody and refused to lick ass. No one could tell them what to do and they got into all sorts of trouble as a result. For these few hardcore individuals, not even the good work of the Youth Project could compensate. But many other youths had been getting into positive things since the Centre opened. Despite the way the system worked against them, they were getting educated and keeping themselves out of trouble, even if it meant staying away from certain friends. 'What bad ah morning can't turn good ah evening' says the old proverb, but the Westview Youth Project was proving that wrong.

The police officers weren't too enthusiastic about their duties that afternoon. Most of them knew the reputation of the Westview Estate and since early morning when they first arrived in the area, tension had been rising tangibly. Westview was one of those locations known to them as 'frontline', which their intelligence told them were sanctuaries for youngsters from the black community to congregate, and that wasn't acceptable. For the youth, the frontline was where they could find out quickly what was going down in the area and who was around. Even the legendary reggae king Bob Marley was renowned to have had the Brixton frontline high on his list of priorities whenever he was in London. People on the frontline always looked cool and relaxed because those few yards of pavement afforded them some slight relief from the constant, overbearing harassment of the local police and its heavy-handed methods. On the frontline, the police were viewed as intruders. They weren't welcome. And they hadn't forgotten the 'bloody good hiding' they had received on Westview two years earlier and were not convinced that the Estate had undergone the much publicised 'transformation'. They were as wary of black youth as the youngsters were of them and mindful that their heavy policing tactics could always lead to more trouble than they could handle.

But duty called. For some inexplicable reason the Princess of Wales was paying a visit to the Estate and she was to be afforded an adequate police presence.

Suddenly, the wail of a police siren could be heard approaching down the main road. In a few moments, the two motorcycle outriders were visible, clearing the road ahead and followed by the two limousines and the police car behind. The convoy rolled into the Estate without much fanfare. Few local people had been told of the Princess' visit, but some press photographers had been tipped off.

Some seconds later the Princess of Wales, tall, slim and attractive, stepped out of the second of the limousines — the door held open for her by her chauffeur — onto the red carpet on which a proudly beaming Rev. Marshall was standing. Accompanied by a flurry of flashes from the trio of major league photographers who had managed to get wind of this unusual royal engagement, the Reverend bowed and told her how delighted they all were that she was able to be there.

By now, some of the residents of the Estate had gathered — their curiosities tickled by the spectacle. On seeing the popular Princess of Wales, many of them applauded and cheered loudly almost despite themselves.

Smiling all the time, the Princess — dressed simply in a canary yellow, matching jacket and skirt cut for the summer, and a broad-brimmed navy blue hat that hid half her face — accompanied the Reverend into the Centre, where the Youth Project's Steering Committee were assembled to meet her.

Everybody was beaming with pride as it had now sunk in that the Princess of Wales really had deemed it important enough to come and officially launch their newly-renovated Centre. Leroy took his turn in line to be introduced to her, smiling broadly. 'I knew she was fit', he told himself admiring, 'but she look criss as well'.

The Princess made her way forward, shaking hands and stopping to chat for a moment or two. Behind her was a group of dignitaries and Detective Sergeant Evans, her personal bodyguard, keeping his eyes peeled, making sure that no undesirables got too close to the Princess. He didn't like the look of the tall guy with the tiny dreadlocks standing waiting to be introduced. But there was nothing he could do about that now.

Finally the Princess got to Leroy.

" 'Nuff respect, Princess," he greeted her.

"I beg your pardon?" she said, not quite catching his words.

"I said 'nuff respect... big up yuhself, I like your style, you know —wicked!"

'Thank you," the Princess said with a warm smile. "So what do you do for the Youth Project?"

"Youth Development Officer," said Leroy. "It's my job to motivate the youngsters in this area, to do the right thing, you know, set up a little business..."

"Oh that must be very interesting. Is that easy?"

"No, not at all... It's a kinda twenty-four-seven, three sixty-five kinda t'ing, you know. The youths out here need all the support they can get; life seems pretty hopeless from their point of view."

The Princess smiled, obviously impressed by the dreadlocked personality in front of her.

"And tell me something," she asked, "how do you get your hair to grow like that?"

Leroy smiled back, his baby locks had often broken down the ice in conversations with white people.

"It's not easy... Maybe I could show you some time..."

The Princess smiled. Reverend Marshall coughed nervously and then turned to introduce the Princess to the two local youngsters standing nervously behind her, who had been chosen to meet the royal guest personally: the Estate's young boffin — a 17-year-old boy dressed in oversize jeans and hooded sweatshirt who had just passed his A-levels two years early and a 16-year-old girl whose hurdling abilities had gained her the occasional place with the Great Britain athletics team.

Leroy had spotted Lyndon looking anxiously over in

his direction. Everything had gone smoothly so far. All they needed now was the last part of his plan to go well. He was banking on the fact that the Princess, as had often been reported, was a bit of a raver. He nodded over at his friend. Lyndon disappeared down the steps to the basement for a moment and then returned and smiled at Leroy with a thumbs up sign.

With a huge smile, Rev. Marshall led the way into the Centre's main hall, its bright yellow walls now draped with flags from Caribbean and African commonwealth countries, interspersed with Union Jacks. At one end of the hall, the entire 24-person Westview Community Gospel Choir were assembled, dressed formally with grey cassocks thrown over their suits and evening dresses. The Princess took her seat amongst the handful of comfortable, cushioned theatre chairs which had been borrowed for the occasion. As soon as she had taken her seat, the Reverend took his place on the platform in front of the Choir. Bowing once more, he turned around to face the choir he was so proud of, and waving his hands fervently, conducted them through a rendition of 'Lift Every Voice And Sing'. The Princess seemed to be enjoying it, flanked by her dignitaries and a few of the Centre's committee members. Her bodyguard was still keeping a watchful eye on the proceedings, obviously 'on duty'.

The Choir, had only got halfway through their performance, when the entire building including the hallway and the stairways erupted with the wail of police sirens coming at full volume out of speakers which had been set up at vantage points all over the Centre.

For a moment, there was confusion around the royal guest. In the main hall where Rev. Marshall was still frantically trying to hold command of the situation by urging his choir with gestures of his hands to sing louder for the benefit of the Princess, the roar through the speakers had made everything else inaudible. The Princess stood rooted to the ground with a look of bemusement on her face. Her personal bodyguard wasn't sure whether the aural assault wasn't part of the programme. He reached for his breast pocket, ready but unable to hear anything down his earpiece. Whilst Rev. Marshall struggled in vain with the Choir, encouraging them to even louder heights, the rest of the Westview Youth Project committee were too shocked by the unexpected interruption to make a move. Only Leroy and Lyndon seemed unbothered.

On cue, the voice of an MC came piercing through the speakers:

"Now hear dis -

You're tuned into the crucial sounds of Kool MC Lesley Lyrics

Comin' atcha straight an' won't try no funny tricks

'Cause whether you're black or whether you're white

Mek we all come together an' unite — y'all

An' special request to the royal princess

Run t'ings inna every contest

An' massive dedication to my older breddah Leroy

Ah you control dis area yah — for years an' years, man!

Come my selector, beg you drop the style an' fashion

With no interruption..."

Without warning, a fast and furious riddim exploded

out of the speakers.

By now all eyes were fixed on Leroy.

"So, you're responsible for this", Rev. Marshall growled at him when he eventually gave up on the conducting and stepped off the stage, the music still blaring. Leroy cupped his ear and shrugged his shoulders as if he couldn't hear the Reverend above all the music. Fortunately for him, the Princess still sat happily, smiling, bobbing her head appreciatively to the music. Leroy smiled. He had been counting on her enjoying it.

"Would you like to come downstairs and see the studio we've built?" he asked the Princess once the music had died down.

"Yes, I'd love to," the Princess said with a smile.

"You ever hear of junglist?"

" 'Junglist'," the Princess repeated, "what's that?"

Leroy led the party downstairs into the basement where a couple of youths were huddled over a mixing desk, tuning up the vocals of a third youth deejaying into a microphone in the glass booth beyond.

"Magic, turn down the sound lickle bit," Leroy told the heavy set youth in the baseball cap.

The youth turned down the volume and looked casually up at the crowd of dignitaries who had packed into the tiny studio. He looked at the Princess and smiled, then nudged his partner at the mixing desk and jerked his head in the direction of the royal. His friend looked over and muttered a barely audible, "Nice!"

"Your majesty, may I present Anthony Carnegie, also known as 'Magic', the boy who invented 'jungle' music," Leroy introduced him proudly.

Magic looked over at the Princess and presented his clenched fist for her to 'touch'. The royal looked puzzled.

"Oh, that's how we shake hands in the community," Leroy said with a shrug of his shoulders. "We touch fists like this."

"Oh that's rather nice." The Princess giggled and 'touched' fists with Magic.

By this time, the next youth who had been rapping in the studio pushed his way into the control room. The Princess congratulated him.

"So how did you invent this 'jungle' music?" the Princess asked.

"Well, it wasn't just me one," Magic admitted coyly, "...we was just sitting down here in the studio, a group of us, and we were playing ragga music, y'know, and a next yout' came down with a tape with some ruff drum samples on it and we started playing about with it, you know, with the mixing and speeding it up, and then Leslie came down and dropped some lyrics on top in a ragga style and everybody said the two things together sound wicked..."

"Well congratulations," the Princess said.

"Yeah, jungle music," Leroy added. "It's the biggest thing out there in clubland."

"I'm a bit of a clubber myself," the Princess admitted, "but I haven't heard of jungle."

"You will soon," Leroy assured her, "but by then, no one will acknowledge Magic as the inventor. Everybody else is gonna make money out of his invention. That's how it is for these kids... That's why they get frustrated."

At that point the taller youth who had been mixing with Magic earlier and who had been observing the royal party quietly, suddenly challenged the Princess.

"If you really wanted to come down here you should have brought some jobs with you for the local youths..."

The comment stunned the assembled party. Rev. Marshall was obviously dismayed.

"Behave yourself, Colin," he hissed, "yuh nuh have no manners?"

The Princess wasn't phased however.

"Yes, I wish I could have brought some jobs. I wish I could help a lot of people, but I'm just a Princess.... what can I do?"

"Well I can arrange for you to come down here again sometime and you can meet more of the youths who use the Centre," Leroy offered. "These kids really need some help from someone like you... someone in your position who could go out and say, yeah, I'm backing these inner city kids who aren't being given the chance but are trying to achieve something."

"That does sound a good idea," the Princess said, "I might just do that. Maybe we could speak about that sometime."

"Yeah you see, what they would really like to do is to get a licence to set up their own radio station... and you could definitely help there..."

The Rev. Marshall decided that he had heard enough.

"Perhaps the Princess would like to see the rest of the Centre...?" he said, leading the way back up the stairs.

The rest of the royal visit to the Centre went much more smoothly. Rev. Marshall managed to maintain a decent distance between Leroy and the Princess and continually flashed the Project's Youth Development Officer some evil looks.

The Princess enjoyed herself at the Centre so much that she stayed much longer than initially planned. So long in fact, that by the time the Princess left the building to climb into her waiting limousine, a sizeable crowd had gathered outside waiting for her. A big cheer went up as she stepped out into the late afternoon sun. She wound down her rear passenger window and waved a royal wave, before being driven off at speed out of the Estate with her police escort.

Leroy watched the motorcade leave and decided to chip before Rev. Marshall threw the wrath of the gospel at him. He hurried away to his car which was parked on the other side of the Centre. As he made his way over, he remembered something. He pulled out his mobile and dialled quickly.

"Yeah Bagga, it's me Leroy... Wha' ah gwan? You pick up Patsy okay?"

Leroy listened unimpressed as his driver explained that the plan had backfired. He had got to Patsy's house in the limousine as they had arranged, to pick her up. When she had realised that Leroy wasn't going to arrive until much later, she had got angry and refused to follow Bagga. They had stood on her doorstep discussing the matter for a few minutes, when this heavy-set yankee guy had arrived and offered to take Patsy out for her birthday instead, and she had agreed.

'Shit!' Leroy thought. That was all he needed.

"Alright Bagga. Respect to the maximum, still. It's not your fault."

He snapped the phone shut and climbed into his car,

heading for Patsy's apartment. It had been an almost perfect day; why did Patsy have to ruin it in this way?

He should have known that Patsy wouldn't go for his plan. To him, it was simple: Patsy wanted to spend her birthday having a picnic at Kew Gardens.

"Let's just take it easy and spend a relaxing day down by the river," she had insisted.

So he had come up with the idea that his friend Bagga, who worked for a wedding car business in Harlesden, would pick her up at midday and drive her out to Kew Gardens and then he would join them late in the afternoon and take over after the Princess had been to the Centre. He had even bought a huge hamper from Harrods for the picnic. Patsy was to have everything she wanted, he just couldn't make it to the picnic on time, that's all. Later he would take Patsy out to dinner at Walsh's — an elegant and expensive restaurant on Charlotte Street in the West End, which he had heard about with excellent recommendations. After dinner, he had planned a romantic movie. They would have spent the rest of the evening snuggled up together in the middle row of some cinema. That's what he had been looking forward to, but now she was with this yankee... What the raas was his game?

Despite the traffic, it only took a quarter of an hour to drive to Shepherd's Bush because Leroy knew all the back streets around White City. There were no parking spaces. He parked half way down the street, climbed out of the BMW with a spring in his step and made his way back to Patsy's flat. He let himself in the two-storey Victorian red-bricked mansion block, and climbed the steps up to her first floor flat two at a time, letting himself in with his keys. It was only then that he realised that he didn't know what he was doing there. Patsy wasn't around and he had no idea when she would be back. He paced up and down amongst the African ornaments in the living room, thinking. There had to be a way of figuring... Then a thought flashed through his mind. Just maybe...

Leroy stepped over to the telephone and with the receiver to his ear, pressed the 'redial' button. He waited as the tone sounded. After three rings a voice answered:

"Speedie Cars, can I help you?"

In his best formal voice, Leroy explained that it was a matter of urgency, one of their cars had driven his sister from her flat earlier that day. She had to be contacted immediately: a family matter of life and death. The voice at the other end sounded dubious, but Leroy sounded so convincing that eventually he got what he wanted.

"Now let me see..." came the voice..."ah, here we are, 2pm pick up for Ms Hines, from Shepherd's Bush, to The Hadleigh Hotel, Park Lane."

In a flash, Leroy was outside in his car, heading for Park Lane. He hadn't considered it through, because his thoughts were grappling with the intense jealousy that raged in the deepest depths of his stomach. Patsy had taken the cab to the American's hotel, there could be only one explanation. Supposing she was inside his room? What was he going to do then? He didn't know how he was going to do it, but he would have to burst in. If there was still a chance of stopping Patsy from making a big mistake, he had to take it.

"I don't see anything wrong with a little bump and grind," J.R. said with a smile. He knew how Patsy would react, because he had tested his opinion on many women before. They always sounded horrified at first and it would take a lot more teasing and coaxing before they would admit that they too saw nothing wrong with it.

J.R. Reynolds had a taste for the finest things in life. Good wine, a good cigar, good food and good women were things he didn't take lightly. Especially good food. He had suggested that they should dine at his hotel, before going on to a performance by the Dance Theatre of Harlem in Covent Garden. He didn't care for ballet much, in fact he knew it was going to be hard staying awake, but it was Patsy's birthday and he remembered how she had earlier mentioned that the thing she missed most in her job was that with all the flying around she never got much chance to go to the ballet any more. Her wish was his command. Besides, he was trying to impress Patsy, and he knew that she would be impressed by his ability to acquire two good seats despite the fact that the performance was sold out. He had paid over the odds for the tickets through the young Asian porter at his hotel, but they were worth every penny. Money was no problem, he had lots of money and nothing would please him more than to spend a good portion of it on this English woman that he liked so much because of her *savoir-faire*, because of her *je ne sais quoi*. They had talked for hours about all kinds of things and the closer he got to her, the more she was making him smile and though he held back because her body language was telling him not to rush things, that it was still too early in their relationship, his body, mind and soul were all burning with a deep desire for her. For J.R. Reynolds, Patsy Hines was a dream come true.

"There's more to sex than just bumping and grinding," Patsy said, taking another sip of champagne. It was her birthday and she intended to enjoy it. Leroy was history. He had let her down once too often; this time she couldn't forgive him. Not only could he not find the time to spend the day with her on her birthday, but he didn't even have the decency to call up and tell her, preferring to send his messenger instead. She wasn't just hurt, she felt insulted too. Unlike Leroy, J.R. seemed to care and had given up his day and important meetings to spend the day with her. Sometimes it was important that someone simply cared.

They had spent the afternoon at Kew Gardens, just as she wanted. The gardens always seemed to relax her, even if it was strange being there with someone other than Leroy. It was peaceful and romantic, the way she wanted her birthday to be. J.R. had talked about boxing excitedly, giving his opinion of all the great heavyweights of the past and concluding that Mike Tyson at his peak was pound — for — pound the best ever.

"Respect where respect's due," he said, "but Tyson would have wiped the floor with the likes of Joe Louis and Sonny Liston not to talk of Foreman, Frazier, Norton and all those other champs. Even Ali... my boyhood hero... I wouldn't have liked to see him face Iron Mike at his peak, because that young brother was mean, you know what I'm saying?"

They had also talked about relationships. J.R. couldn't understand why she had put up with Leroy's behaviour for so long and to be honest, looking at it in the cold light of day, neither could she.

"Man shall not live by bump and grind alone," Patsy continued whimsically. "That's why men can never understand women, we're more complex. Feelings complicate things. I spent so many nights awake trying to explain that to Leroy, but he just didn't get it. In most relationships, when something somewhere is wrong... it is usually the man."

Though technically she was still in a relationship with Leroy and would be until she formally 'broke off', Patsy couldn't help thinking that if she was going to have a scene with anyone, it could easily be J.R. He was a really nice guy: handsome, a bit of a hunk and although he had a tendency to brag, he took time out to boost her confidence also. The way she felt now after three glasses of champagne, she wouldn't even mind sleeping with the guy, after all it was her birthday and it felt good allowing herself to be desired. Of course she wouldn't sleep with him. No sex on a first, second or third date, that was the way she had always been. She didn't want any man thinking she was easy. She sipped at the champagne some more. It was fun going out with J.R. as a friend and that was the way it was staying, however bad things had got with Leroy.

J.R. smiled. Bumping and grinding was no big deal, he insisted again. "It's been going on since the beginning of time." But she was right of course, he added, "to touch a woman's soul, you gotta have feelings. But remember, love is like a candy on the shelf. If you want a taste, you have to help yourself..."

"That's nonsense. Total nonsense..." Patsy said,

throwing her head back in laughter. "Why can't men say what they mean and mean what they say?"

'Yes,' J.R. thought to himself, 'I shall have this woman'. He didn't know if he was allowing himself to be seduced by the English accent too much or whether it was her feisty attitude that he liked, but he didn't feel like doing anything else but spending all his time with her. Her man had to be crazy for not taking care of her, not satisfying her. When you satisfy your woman, there's no reason for her to stay up half the night awake. This Leroy guy didn't know what he had, so he had to lose her. That was his own fault for not realising that his woman was one of a kind. But Leroy's loss was going to be his gain. He would show this 'rasta' guy how to treat a woman.

Eventually, once they had finished their meals, J.R. admitted that he wanted to sleep with her. Patsy was expecting as much. She rarely met men who were happy with going out for a friendly meal without wanting sex at the end of it. Patsy declined without hesitation. J.R. asked her why.

"Well, why do you want to sleep with me?"

"Because you can make me happy, and I can make you happy... I know what you're going through, your boyfriend's..."

"You don't know what I'm going through," Patsy laughed. "How could you, you hardly know me."

"But you're a woman, you've been hurt in your relationship. Believe me I know what a woman needs in this situation, some good, good loving..."

"But all women are not the same..."

"A woman, is a woman, is a woman," J.R. insisted

with a smile.

If it wasn't for the champagne, Patsy may have thought that J.R. was treading on dangerous ground but it was her birthday and she simply wanted to have fun.

"For the time being anyway," she said, "I *am* in a relationship..."

"But I thought you said...?"

"That's between me and Leroy..."

Patsy sighed. She didn't want to be reminded of Leroy. After three years, breaking up wouldn't be easy, but since failing to show up for her birthday, Leroy was only half the man he used to be in her eyes. She had put his loving to the test and he had failed miserably. Leroy's problem was that he couldn't see that he mixed up love with material things. He thought his woman needed diamonds and rings of 18 carat gold more than she needed a supportive hand to help lift her to a higher ground.

"You fight your natural feelings though, don't you?" J.R. said. "I've noticed that about you. It's like suppressing your passions and a woman should never suppress her passions.

"I don't suppress my passions."

"So what are you going to do about your situation? You've got a man who treats you like he doesn't want you and you've got a man like me, who wants to take you higher, further than any one of your jumbo jets have ever taken you. How can I prove what I feel about you?"

Patsy felt that that would be carrying things a bit too far. She advised J.R. to be patient and take his time. If he really wanted to prove anything to her he might yet get his chance. If she made things too easy for him he wouldn't appreciate it.

J.R. shrugged his shoulders. Patsy was putting up a whole lot of resistance, but he could sense that they were going to work things out.

Leroy parked around the corner from the luxury hotel and jumped out of the BMW, there was no time to waste. Within moments he was standing in the hotel foyer, his mind ticking all the time. His eyes scanned the surroundings quickly and settled on the young, Asian hotel porter.

"Yes star, respect!" Leroy walked up to him. "I need some information."

The porter eyed him suspiciously.

"I'm looking for a yank... big man, fat, jeri curls, moustache... flash dresser..."

"Yeah, I know him..." the porter confided in a thick south London accent, "what kinda information you looking for?"

"You know his room number?"

"I can't jus' give you that kinda information, this is a hotel, you know."

Leroy had already dipped into his money belt and pulled out a £50 note from the wad. He tucked it into the porter's red waistcoat jacket.

"Hold some change."

The porter pulled the note out of his waistcoat, examined it briefly and with a neat fold tucked it into his trouser pocket.

"What information exactly d'you want?" he asked.

"The American guy — what's his name?"

"J.R... J.R. Reynolds... Room 547... but he's out."

"Did he go out by himself?"

"No, he was with this black chick, nice you know, elegant, tall..."

"You know where they went?" Leroy asked urgently.

The Asian youth looked about him.

"Hang about," he said and stepped out of the hotel's glass doors to converse with the top-hatted doorman. After a moment, the porter returned.

"He wants some change as well," he said.

Leroy shrugged and pulled another £50 note from his tightly wrapped roll of banknotes and handed it over.

"He says they got into a taxi about an hour ago, to take them to the Opera House, Covent Garden.

Leroy thought for a minute. Then he pulled off another £50 note from his wad and tucked it into the porter's waistcoat.

"I don't care how you do it, but any calls coming in to this American guy between now and tomorrow afternoon, just make sure he doesn't get 'em. Tell the caller he's out, whatever you want..."

The porter pulled out the crisp note and examined it.

"This is alright for me, mate," he said, "but the woman on switchboard's going to want something also..."

Leroy shrugged and pulled off another note. Without explanation he ripped it in half through the middle, then handed one half to the porter.

"Okay, if you do the job right, you'll get the other half tomorrow afternoon."

The porter said it was fine, knowing that the half Leroy had was no good to him by itself.

"So this woman he was with, she's your woman is it?" the porter asked.

"Who wants to know?"

"It's just because they seemed to be getting a bit intimate, you know..."

Leroy didn't need to hear any more. He made his way quickly out of the hotel. Outside, he gunned the engine of the BMW and steered furiously out of the parking space and pointed the vehicle in the direction of Covent Garden.

Several things were going through his mind, as he raced down Park Lane, dodging in and out of the evening traffic, unsure whether he was too late, unsure whether Patsy had allowed the yank to go too far. The mood she was in, he wasn't confident that he could afford to allow the American the opportunity. This American needed two serious slaps to get the message across once and for all that Patsy wasn't available. The man was waging a serious campaign to get Patsy and Leroy wasn't doing much to stop him. If he wasn't careful, he could lose his woman and he really didn't want that. Definitely not to some yank. If he and Patsy couldn't keep their relationship going that was one thing, but he didn't want to lose the best woman he had ever had for no good reason.

"So what did you think of the performance?" Patsy asked as she and J.R. pushed their way through the hundreds of people packed into the foyer of the Opera House, at the end of the performance by the Harlem dance troupe.

J.R. thought carefully before he answered. He knew it wouldn't go down too well if he was honest and said that it was the most boring two hours he had ever spent. So he said something about how funny it was to see men in tights.

"Those guys wouldn't last two minutes in my old neighbourhood in the Bronx..."

His first time at the ballet had been as boring as he had always imagined it would be. Patsy made it tolerable. He was trying real hard to make sure she gave him that break he was looking for, because boyfriend or no boyfriend, he was going to do his uttermost to make sure that they spent the night together. Tonight might be the last chance. He was going back to the States in the morning and Patsy was leaving on a long haul flight to Sydney. So although he had struggled to stay awake for the duration of the 'Nutcracker', he knew that it was all for a good cause.

"So what now?" J.R. asked as they stood on the pavement outside. "Shall we go to a bar, or back to my hotel for some more champagne?"

"No, no more champagne..."

Patsy had had a great time, but she didn't want things to become awkward between them. She had thought about it right through the last section of the ballet performance. She didn't want to do anything silly and end up regretting this birthday. Even though she was flying off tomorrow and J.R. was too, there would be many more chances to meet if they both wanted to. Today just wasn't the right time.

"You shouldn't be going home to an empty flat..." J.R. started, "this is your birthday. Let's just get a cab to my hotel. There's a really nice private bar in there... just come back for one drink. That doesn't mean I'm asking you to stay overnight —unless you want to of course..."

Patsy looked up at J.R. It was great to feel wanted and desired. Maybe this guy only had one thing on his mind, but at least he was making an effort.

"We'll see, shall we?" she said, taking his arm but giving nothing away. "I'll come to the hotel for a drink... just one drink. There's only two hours left of my birthday and I'm flying off tomorrow. Let's just have one nice drink together and leave it at that. Okay?"

"Your wish is my command," said J.R., executing a mock bow and beaming all over his face. He stuck two fingers in his mouth and whistled for a taxi. "The Hadleigh Hotel!" he told the driver, then held the door open for Patsy in true gentleman style.

"Oh thank you!" said Patsy with a smile as she stepped into the back of the cab.

That was the last thing she said to J.R. that night. The next moment, the taxi door had slammed shut and the cab was rolling away towards the Strand.

"Hey, stop the taxi!" Patsy cried out, turning to see J.R. standing helplessly on the street, waving his arms frantically for the cab to stop. "You've driven off without my friend."

The taxi driver didn't seem to hear her cries. Patsy banged on his glass window.

"Stop the cab... hey what's going on?"

It was only then that she noticed the tiny baby dreadlocks underneath the cab driver's flat cap.

"Leroy?" she asked puzzled, "if that's you Leroy... if that's you..."

The cab driver turned around and flashed a cheeky, gold-toothed smile.

"You never thought you'd get so much excitement on your birthday, did you?"

"Leroy, you bastard," Patsy pushed back the glass separating driver and passenger, pulled off his cap and slapped him over the head with it. "Turn this cab around and take me back to where I was... this isn't funny!!"

Leroy struggled to gain control of the taxi whilst dodging Patsy's blows. He could hardly see where he was going but she didn't seem to care.

"I ain't laughing," Leroy said, suddenly serious.

"Then turn around or stop the cab this minute and let me get out."

"So that you can go back to that yank? Patsy, this is your birthday, we're supposed to be together. Why d'you wanna go and diss the programme like that?"

"Diss the programme?! Who's dissing the programme? You stood me up — again! I can't believe that I fall for it every time. But no more, Leroy. I've had enough. You don't have time to spend with me on my birthday and I don't have time to spend with you in my life, so let me out here."

Leroy had to play clever, dodging all the red lights. If he was forced to stop the taxi, he knew Patsy would jump out. She seemed really angry. He didn't want a scene outside the Opera House so he had come up with the idea of the disguise to spirit Patsy away. The black cabbie waiting to pick up fares outside the Savoy said it had been a quiet night and was happy to lease his vehicle to Leroy for a couple of hours at £200 an hour.

"Patsy, ease off with the pressure will you."

"You started it," Patsy said coldly, "this is kidnap you know... I hope you know that." She hadn't wanted her birthday to end up like this.

"What else was I supposed to do?" Leroy asked. "Was I supposed to just stand back while you were going off with him?"

"Look Leroy, we were supposed to spend the day together, remember? It's my birthday. You think that by sending flowers and a car you've got no more obligations? You can't even tell me that you're not going to make it. I've had enough of it. I want you out of my life. I'm tired of flying back, always looking forward to being with you and then coming home and you're not there because you can't find the time."

"Look, take it easy," Leroy insisted, "I didn't know it was bugging you that much. I'll change, okay. I mean, I'll do anything for you, you know that Patsy."

Like Patsy said, she wasn't having any of it. A leopard couldn't change its spots, nor Leroy change his ways. Their relationship, if it continued, was always going to be part-time. She felt that she deserved more than second best.

CHAPTER 7

The BMW convertible pulled up into the car park of the superstore. Leroy pulled on his darkers and stepped out. It had been one of those hot, bright summer days which were usually rare, but had seemed in abundance this year. He made his way back towards the entrance to the car park and stopped by an old style Datsun parked up with its boot open and packed with all sorts of goods. The vendor's eyes brightened up when she saw Leroy.

"Yes ruffneck don," the large girl with the dollar earrings greeted, "wha' ah gwan?"

"Safe y'know, Sharon."

Sharon was one of Leroy's most successful street vendors. Her 'pitch' outside the Ladbroke Grove superstore was definitely a lucrative one and always brought in top sales, even if it was only selling out of the back of a car.

Leroy had built up a distribution network over the last few years, unmatched in black British enterprise. Through a series of formerly unemployed youth selling his products on the street at selected sites all over London, he had been able to push product at a fast rate. He now had twenty vendors selling his goods at fifty percent commission; all sorts of products, from black interest posters and calenders to certain arts and crafts and the occasional line in clothing — either batty riders or trainers — and perfumes and incense. Also available was a complete set of X Press books including *Baby Father*, *Cop Killer*, *O.P.P*, *Jamaica Inc.* and *Lick Shot*, all of which were perennial bestsellers.

Leroy was of the opinion that if his mind could imagine something, it wasn't impossible. He had long banished the word 'impossible' from his vocabulary. Like he always told his vendors, "You gotta have faith in yourself, or you won't achieve anything. Just believe you can do it, and you can. Be the best! Be the best!" So many black youth had lost the inner convictions, that right mental attitude, that fire in the guts, that leads to success.

He had now managed to assemble a nice little crew together to sell his goods: young black youths who refused to be slaves to their circumstances; who believed that they were better than they were given credit for and were taking the necessary steps to change their circumstances.

"Nothing comes from doing nothing," was Leroy's favourite motto to his salesmen. If you spent all day thinking about your dickie, all you are at the end of it is one big dickie. But if you wanted to earn more money than you were currently earning, you had to work bloody hard.

"So how's sales going today?"

"Not too bad, you know," Sharon answered, "well you know how Saturday runs — always good sales on a Saturday."

"You sell any of those trainers yet?"

"Yeah I was going to talk to you about them, boss. Mikes? You sure they weren't supposed to be Nikes?"

"So they're not selling?" Leroy guessed.

"Man I can't give 'em away. Ask yourself, would you buy a pair of trainers called Mikes?"

Leroy had to admit that he wouldn't and he couldn't see many of the local youth doing so either.

"Just keep trying," he insisted. "Knock a pound off the price, do what you've got to do, just sell 'em. We've got a lot of them to shift."

Leroy spent a minute improving the presentation of the goods in the boot, before making his way back to the car park and his BMW.

"Leroy!" he spun around as he heard his name called out.

"Leroy!"

It was Donna, one of Patsy's friends, struggling to push a shopping cart laden with produce, whilst dragging along her misbehaving young daughter who couldn't have been more than two years old.

"Yeah Donna, what you sayin'?" Leroy said giving her a brief hug. "When is it due?"

Donna beamed a huge smile of pride and looked down at her heavy stomach.

"Any day now... and it's twins this time!"

"Twins! Bwoy you and that husband of yours must be working overtime."

Leroy took control of the trolley, Donna had enough on her hands trying to keep her young daughter — who had only just realised that her mother had no intention of returning to the store to get any "choc-late" and had

105

begun bawling.

"Yes, I have a man who works overtime. That's better than some man I can mention," she said with a knowing wink. "Zora! Behave yourself. I told you already, I'm not buying you any chocolate so that you can mash up your teeth!"

This seemed to upset her daughter even more and the child was silent for a moment as she gathered as much air as she could into her lungs. This was only the calm before the storm; suddenly Zora let out an almighty wail which attracted the attention of almost everyone in the superstore car park — some of whom, by the looks on their faces, suspected that the mother had assaulted the young child.

"I got a call last week from Patsy in Buenos Aires — bwoy dat gyal can fly, eenh? — she asked me to water her plants while she's away."

"So I suppose she told you?" Leroy asked.

The child, now sucking her thumb contentedly, had quietened down immediately her mother threatened to abandon her in the car park. Chocolate was good, but not that good.

"Well you know how we women are..." Donna said conspiratorially, "we tell each other everything."

"Yeah, I bet."

It had been almost three weeks now, yet Leroy hadn't told anybody about himself and Patsy splitting up; he simply didn't like people knowing his and Patsy's personal business. He still hoped that she was just angry and that they would get back together again as soon as she came back home. But she had returned from Australia, changed her door locks and gone off again,

106

without accepting any of his calls and refusing to open the door for him when he went around to her flat.

After his daring getaway in the taxi, Leroy had driven Patsy home. She was determined not to allow Leroy to ruin her birthday, and tried all evening to contact J.R. at his hotel, but was told repeatedly that there was "no reply from Mr Reynolds' room." She thought it odd that he hadn't called her either, but it wasn't until the next morning that she discovered that the ringer switch on her phone was in the 'off' position, and her suspicions turned to Leroy. When she later discovered that Leroy had paid the telephonist at the hotel to not put any calls through to J.R., she was livid.

"So, are you happy now you're on your own? Isn't that what you always wanted? Now you can take care of all your runnings without any interference from Patsy. You must be happy about how that turned out."

Leroy grimaced. Donna already knew too much about his business. She also knew that he wasn't feeling too good. He had considered his situation for more than two weeks now, hoping each night that Patsy would call. Finally, one night, he took the decision that well, if that's the way she wanted to play it, fine. It was going to spur him on to become even richer and more successful than she could imagine and he would make sure she regretted splitting up with him. By morning however, he had decided that making her regret things was no good to him if at the end of the day she was married to somebody else. He wanted Patsy, he wanted her as his woman, she was the only woman he was interested in. With her he always felt cool, relaxed, he could talk to her about anything, he could open up to her, she knew everything about him. If only he could pull off this radio licence, it would be like a licence to print money. All he needed was the permission to run his own legal station and Patsy would surely see that everything he did was for her. He'd be ready to settle down then, get married and start a family together with her.

"She left me, how am I going to feel good about that?" Leroy said finally.

"Yeah, but you're a man," Donna teased, "you can get over it."

"Seriously D., she say anything to you?"

"Like what?"

"About us. Does she still want to split up?"

Donna looked Leroy up and down as he helped her load her Micra full with shopping.

"Me sorry fe you, you know Leroy. Your woman's thrown you out and you're asking me whether she still wants to split up? Men like you never really understand anything your women are saying, do you?"

Leroy listened. She was right of course. The relationship was over... but there had to be a way?

"So, you don't think..." he began.

"No chance," Donna concluded firmly.

"So, you speak to her?"

"I'll be seeing her when she gets back."

"Well, say 'hi'."

"I'll do better than that, I'll tell her that you looked miserable and sick and that you've lost a lot of weight... You do want her back don't you?"

She winked at Leroy. He caught the drift and smiled.

"Anything you can do, Donna."

"Yes, well, you're lucky you have a good friend in

me," she teased, helping her daughter into the baby seat at the back and then climbing in herself.

"You men," Donna said as she drove away, "one day you'll learn that your woman is your most valuable asset and then you'll take care of her."

Leroy smiled as she drove away, now more confident about things. If anyone could change Patsy's mind, it was Donna. And she had always liked him, so he knew she would do anything she could. He climbed into the BMW and took the top down. He flicked on the stereo. There was silence. He checked the dial again and re-tuned. Still there was no sound on the Groove FM frequency. Leroy calculated. He had a feeling he knew what that meant. He pulled out his mobile and dialled the digits hurriedly.

"Lyndon, what's up, man, what's up with the station?"

His partner's voice came down the line. Hadn't Leroy heard, the station got busted by the DTI — accompanied by a heavy police presence. Lesley and Magic got charged, but they were okay. All the equipment was confiscated, as well as a couple of hundred records. Magic was already working on a new transmitter, but it would take a few days before they were back on the air, maybe a week.

"Shit!" Leroy exclaimed. "Tell Magic to pull out all the stops... get the station back on... There's too much advertising money at stake."

"We also need a new venue," Lyndon added. "Reverend Marshall went crazy when he heard about it. For a preacher man he's learned to cuss good when anybody mentions your name."

Leroy smiled to himself, he couldn't have expected anything less from the Reverend.

"What we need," Lyndon continued, "is a raid-proof location to broadcast from... we need somewhere on the twentieth floor of some block of flats, and we need bars at the door like the dealers have... and we need dogs, a couple of pitbulls in case any DTI bwoy try test we."

"What we need," Leroy countered, "is a legal licence. That's where the money is. Look how much Choice an' Sex FM an' dem stations charge in ads, man. I'm tired of ducking and diving and babylon, man, an' picking up scraps for our troubles."

"Yeah man, that's outta order," Lyndon agreed. "You were supposed to be controlling that side of things — the legal business. You hear from the Princess yet?"

"No man, I shoulda known the woman wasn't going to get back, man. She didn't even bother taking my address."

"The woman dissed you, man. But you shoulda made sure you got her number."

"I don't think Princesses just give out their numbers, you know Lyndon."

It didn't matter to Lyndon, he should have asked anyway. If Leroy had been a real cocks man like he was, he wouldn't have missed the opportunity.

Leroy hung up, shifted the car into gear and pulled out of the car park.

CHAPTER 8

The dark blue Mercedes purred out of Buckingham Palace through the side entrance, followed as ever by the black Rover. At the wheel of the Mercedes, the Princess of Wales was in defiant mood. She had spent the last two hours in one of the private wings of the Palace with her estranged husband. She had agreed to this attempt at reconciliation with the hope that there might still be something to salvage from her marriage. It had only taken her a few minutes to realise that there wasn't. The Prince of Wales had been his normal self, stiff and very English. Like the rest of his family he was unable to chill out, not even in private. That had been the problem with their marriage, she concluded. In truth, marriage into the royal family had not been the great fairy tale, 'that every young school schoolgirl dreams about'. Far from it, she had married into a family of rules and tradition and regulations, but little love.

"Nice of you to come," he had greeted her when she arrived at the appointed time earlier that morning. She could see in his eyes that he still felt uncomfortable with domestic conversation. He who talked so confidently to people he didn't know all around the world, found it painful to look in his wife's eyes and be frank for a change.

"How have you been?" she had asked, showing as much interest as she could muster.

"I've been busy, you know, the same old duties here and there," he answered stiffly. His mother had encouraged them to try and meet up "without prejudice" and see if they could work something out between them, "For the sake of the crown".

"Of course, I've missed not having the kids around." the Prince continued.

"Okay, what else?" the Princess asked impatiently.

"Look here," Charles continued, "I know that things haven't been exactly blissful between us but I'd like to keep the family together if possible. We loved each other once and I'm sure that we could still find it in us to love one another again. What do you say to us giving it another go?"

"But we haven't worked anything out. We should be talking about why I left you before deciding to get back together again!"

The Princess' voice was filled with obvious frustration. The Prince's upbringing had taught him that he could always get his own way without working for it, after all he was the future King of the United Kingdom. But this was different. His wife was one of the many people in the country unimpressed by his title.

"I'm sorry," the Prince said hurriedly. "Of course, we should discuss your grievances. Please go ahead. What have you been so upset about?"

"Take a look at yourself, look at us, we're not the same two people who married each other ten years ago.

112

Can't you see that?"

Charles looked puzzled. No, he couldn't see that his wife didn't want the same things that he wanted. He was the heir to the throne. Heirs to the throne got married by arrangement, not because of love.

"Please, think about the family, think about the children," he implored her.

The Prince knew that the whole business of the Princess of Wales fleeing the nest could result in a constitutional crisis. The whole thing could get out of hand and turn ugly. A similar thing had happened to his great-uncle which had resulted in abdication.

"The country depends on you to take your position at my side as Queen," he insisted, "you must do your duty."

The Princess of Wales was the most popular member of the royal family, and she knew it. She had a good hand, but her husband held some cards also. Already, the church was up in arms about their separation. The Princess sighed. It always came down to duty with her husband.

"What about how I feel about the whole thing? Why should I continue in a marriage that is not making me happy? I don't want to be married to you anymore. I want a divorce."

Prince Charles finally lost his patience and decided to spell it out plainly.

"You will never get a divorce," he assured her. "A wife cannot divorce the Prince of Wales. That is an act of treason. I can divorce you, but not the other way around, and you'd have to do something pretty embarrassing before I would even think of divorcing you." He laughed loudly. "Something *really* embarrassing."

The Mercedes sped on through Knightsbridge, the black Rover tailgating it. It was midday and the streets were now filled with taxis. It always made Evans, her bodyguard, nervous when the Princess got in a temper and went zooming off through the centre of town. It was always a security risk when she was in this mood; she was even smoking cigarettes which she should never do in public!

The sleek Mercedes pulled up to the traffic lights. In the next lane, the two Greeks in the old Ford Capri turned, smiling lecherously at the attractive brunette at the wheel of the dark-blue limousine. She looked good enough to eat and was obviously rich. As they dreamt of the possibilities, the lights changed to 'green' and the Mercedes lurched forward with a screech of its wheels and disappeared in the distance.

Diana lit another cigarette. The two men in the Capri obviously didn't recognise her. She was happy about that, the wig always did the trick. People always imagined her as a blonde; all she had to do was wear a dark wig and some dark glasses and she could go virtually anywhere as a regular citizen. She laughed to herself. She wasn't into men with gold medallions and hairy chests, but she would have enjoyed seeing the shock on the face of the two men if she had pulled off the wig. Back in the old days, she would have pulled a stunt like that without thinking twice about it. But she was a member of the royal family now and the years had taken their toll. She had lost that sparkle, that youthful *joie de vivre* which once lit up her face. Her friends were always remarking on how bored she seemed nowadays, and they were right. If only she could revive the carefree spirit she once had.

The Princess had been driving for hours. It was one of those mid-summer evenings when the cool evening breeze made a welcome change from the blazing daytime sun and romantic couples walked arm-in-arm at a leisurely pace enjoying the magic in the air. It seemed as if the whole of London was in love. 'Except me,' the Princess thought grimly.

In the black Rover that still tailed her, Evans couldn't figure out what the Princess was playing at. She had driven through some 'dodgy' areas of London, areas where he wouldn't have felt too comfortable driving through without his trusted regulation Browning automatic at his side. It was his duty to protect the Princess, not to query her about where she felt like driving. Anyway, she was too strong-headed to argue with.

The Princess lit another cigarette — a bad habit she had picked up with all the stress in her life. She steered confidently, in and out of the traffic and turned left at Tower Bridge, heading south for no particular reason. She simply needed this long drive to clear her head, away from all the troubles of royal life.

She couldn't see any point in still being married to the Prince. He didn't even care about her anymore. The whole thing was a charade, but he refused to give her a divorce. Now when she thought back to the beginning of their courtship, she remembered that he had once joked that it was treason for a wife to try and divorce the future King of England, but she had thought that it was just that — a joke. Well, it was no joke now, but she didn't know what to do about it.

She tuned the radio, trying to pick up her favourite station. Even though she rarely got a chance to go clubbing nowadays, she liked to keep informed with what was going on by tuning in to Sex FM, the popular dance music station broadcasting out of North London. But she couldn't find Sex, because on its frequency instead was another station, more raw, more rough, more amateurish, but yes, more exciting. And she recognised the music also, she just couldn't remember what it was called.

The deejay shouted out some requests:

"To Beverly up in Wood Green, receiving us loud and clear

To Janet over there in the West London side of things, she says that these sounds are wicked and wicked and wicked and wicked and WACKAD!!

Big up all the Paradise crew, the Garage massive and big up Samantha who says she's itching all over for a touch of jungle fever...JUNGLIST crew make some noise!!!!"

That was it, the Princess remembered, 'jungle' music. She turned her radio up loud and tried to imagine how anybody could dance to a beat that fast. But she couldn't resist the music. There was something exciting about it, something seductive. She turned the car stereo up even louder. Now she remembered where she had first heard 'jungle' — at the Centre she had officially opened over in West London a few weeks earlier; where she had met the handsome black man with the Soul II Soul haircut. She had thought about him several times since meeting him, wondered what kind of life he led, if he had a woman, if he was happy. He seemed such a nice guy. She had also thought about what one of the kids had said to her about not having brought any jobs with her to the Centre. But what could she do? Ordinary people really didn't understand that a member of the royal family didn't have much power in influencing matters like that. She thought about the charming black guy again and came up with an idea.

Lord Matthew Percy was a rebel royal. Although he was the heir to a multi-million pound fortune, he was more likely to be found hanging out in black neighbourhoods than on his father's country estate. Since an earlier trip to Jamaica, he had got hooked with the reggae vibe and now considered himself an honorary rastaman stepping through babylon. Many other royals begrudged him his street cred, as unlike them he felt comfortable moving around any section of London without a bodyguard, but his unenviable police record was another matter. He was also good friends with the Princess of Wales, with whom he had shared a nanny when they were much younger. In her view, he was the ideal person to carry a message on her behalf to the Westview Youth Project.

It was a Wednesday morning when the rebel royal arrived at Westview, an opened can of Tennants in his hand. As usual a posse of youths were standing at the Craven Park entrance to the Estate, just loafing. They eyed the white man suspiciously. The fact that he raised

117

his hand in a friendly gesture made them even more suspicious. Matthew felt no way, he was used to it. He always took a macabre pleasure in sticking out like a sore thumb — with a pale white face and dressed in a white shirt and white khakis.

He walked on towards the old school building that housed the Project. Outside, a couple of girls were taking a quick cigarette break.

"Good morning," Matthew greeted them, "could you tell me where I might find..." he pulled out a folded slip from his shirt pocket and read the scribbled note.

"...Leroy Massop."

"What do you want with Leroy?" the larger of the two girls with the oversize 'dollar' earrings in her ears said, a hostile look on her face.

"I've got a message for him," the rebel royal said, taking a swig from his can of brew.

"Well give it here..." the girl stretched out her hand.

"No, I can't, it's very important that I give it to him personally."

The girl looked at her friend and kissed her teeth. The other girl raised her eyebrows as if to say, 'dyam fool'.

"Well he's not here, so either you give me the message, or you can forget it."

"Look, maybe I could buy you ladies lunch?" Matthew said.

"Is alright," the big girl said, negatively. "Do you want me to give Leroy a message or don't you?"

Matthew realised that he wasn't going to get much change out of the women. At least they knew Leroy. He tore off a corner of the slip and scribbled down his name and home number. If he hadn't heard from Leroy by the next day, he would check back to the Centre.

"Please make sure he gets this number; it is a matter of national importance."

The two girls gave Matthew a quizzical look, wondering why he was talking in riddles.

Leroy got the message pretty quickly. He was sitting on the barbershop chair, his head tilted back and a clean white napkin around his neck and shaving gel on his face and throat. He had told Fitzroy to give him a shave and to touch the sides and back of his head a little also. As always, Leroy expected nothing but the best from his regular barber so there was no need to look in the mirror until the job was done.

Sharon had called him on his mobile as soon as the white guy had slipped her his number. At the sound of the tone, Leroy flicked open the mobile, his head pointed to the ceiling in the barber salon.

"What did he want?" he asked down the line.

"That's what I was trying to find out," Sharon replied, "but he wouldn't say... he said something about a national emergency."

"You sure he wasn't the bull man?"

"Not unless they've got some really good undercover..."

That was good enough for Leroy. He ended the conversation, then dialled the number his vendor had given him, while Fitzroy shaved under his chin with a cut-throat.

Leroy had kept a low profile from the Centre since his boys got busted on air, just until things cooled down, but those who knew him well always knew how to get hold of him anyway.

His visit to the barber's over, Leroy was back in his car. He dialled the number again. Once more there was only a brief answering message. He snapped his phone shut, put the BMW into gear and headed north. He followed the road out onto the North Circular, where he took a right turn and headed for his destination in North Finchley.

It was the first real chance that Leroy had had to test the car out. He pushed hard on the gas pedal and smiled contentedly as the speedometer dial shot up to the hundred mark. The car handled like a dream on the dual carriageway, taking the road with little vibration of the steering wheel and with hardly a sound coming from the engine. It was at times like this that he felt the power of being successful. He could afford a luxury car now, but he rarely took time out to enjoy it. It was like his relationship with Patsy, he really wanted to enjoy it but he just didn't have time at the moment.

The blue convertible pulled up outside the red-bricked high Victorian walls. Leroy looked up at the sign, still deliberating as to whether he should go in or not. He considered a little more, before slipping the BMW into first and easing his way through the gates.

Visiting the hospital was one chore Leroy would rather have avoided. He rarely went there. In fact it had been such a long time since he was last there that he had decided that he must visit his father today come what may.

Errol Massop had never quite got over the death of his wife Winnie. She had been the backbone of his life and when she passed away of a chronic asthma attack four years previously, Errol had fallen apart. Leroy still felt guilty about the whole thing. He should have realised that his father couldn't cope with the grief on his own, while dealing with the various debts her death had incurred, but he was busy doing other things and his father never once asked for help. Before Leroy knew what was going on, his father had re-mortgaged the house he had worked half his life for, to some loan sharks to pay for his wife's burial. Within a few months of the loan, the Stock Market crashed and interest rates quadrupled overnight. Without a job, Errol Massop was unable to meet the repayments on his loan and lost his house, which was his past, present and future. From that moment on things went downhill for him. Officers at Harrow Road police station were the first to diagnose a breakdown after Mr Massop entered their reception late at night totally naked.

Leroy looked his father up and down. Somehow he was sure that the old man knew who he was, even though his father no longer acknowledged him. The doctors claimed it was due to amnesia caused by the breakdown, but Leroy wasn't so sure. Something made him feel that his father couldn't face his son, which hurt Leroy even more. They were sitting together in the ward's television room, Errol's attention concentrated on the Australian soap opera on the set. It always saddened Leroy to be here. To see the man he had worshipped and obeyed as a youngster reduced to an autistic heap, expressionless in front of the television, always brought him to tears.

His father had always been a winner who never quit

,thing and expected more good out of life than bad. He had no time for a negative outlook and anytime he got knocked back he would simply pick himself up, dust himself off and bounce right back only a little worse for wear. Errol Massop had been a dreamer who dreamt big dreams and encouraged his son to do the same. But now he had lost everything, he no longer dreamt.

Leroy wiped a tear away with the back of his hand as he left the hospital, feeling worse than when he went in. If only his father would talk to him, maybe they could work things out. Maybe Leroy could look after him, maybe his father could get better... if he would only acknowledge his son.

Leroy drove out of the quiet hospital grounds slowly and pointed the BMW back in the direction of Ladbroke Grove, thinking of all the things he would do for his father when he got the money. He would buy the house back for him, the very same house which had been repossessed, and he would send his father on a long holiday to Jamaica, with all the private care he needed to undertake such an endeavour. He would make sure that the rest of his father's days would be comfortable and trouble free.

Errol Massop had always been his son's role model. Everything that Leroy had achieved today was due to his father's influence. If it wasn't for his father he'd still be working for someone else as he had done when he first left school. His job as a welder had been okay, but his father kept reminding him that, "Those who work for someone and receive money in return are always underpaid, no matter how much money they earn." One day Leroy didn't go into work but stayed at home daydreaming of the things he wanted most in life — to start his own business and earn a lot of money. He didn't return to that job again, but stayed at home outlining his plans for achieving his goals. First he needed money but his appeals fell on deaf ears at the listening bank and everywhere else he turned to. Swallowing a large slice of humble pie, he took a job at McDonald's for six months, serving up hamburgers and lived like a monk saving nearly every penny he earned. This was part of life's challenge his father had told him — things get tough sometimes and life tends to favour those who know how to deal with the tough going. Massop senior had even shined shoes, and cleaned out toilets in his day. By example Leroy learned in the cold-blooded academy of ghetto streets, that suffering is inevitable and necessary for an aspiring businessman and not everybody could take it. Of the three types of people in the world: the wills, the wonts and the cants, the second oppose everything, the third fail in everything and the first achieve everything. Leroy was definitely a 'will'.

His father had taught him to think quick on his feet:

"If you're slow making up your mind you'll be slow making and carrying out decisions," Errol always said. "And you have to be ready to take your chance when it arises, otherwise you'll look ridiculous. A great occasion is worth as much as you've prepared for of it. Preparation is the key. It means becoming so good, so competent at what you're doing, that you actually force the success to come your way. You don't have to be a genius to make money, but you have to use what little knowledge you have. And if you're not getting better, you're getting worse. You have to think like a prince, act like a prince, talk like a prince and one day you will become a prince."

Through his father, Leroy had learned the mental requirements for financial success and confidence. He now understood the power of creative imagination. There was no goal too great nor dream too high for him, as long as his mind could conceive and believe, he could achieve it.

"Africans built the pyramids and all the scientists, mathematicians and the geometricians say that that was impossible. So they call the pyramids one of the seven wonders of the world."

Nothing was impossible, Leroy agreed. So before he made his way to the hamburger restaurant every morning, he would devote a few minutes when he woke up each morning to some creative thinking — potential business ideas and how to increase profits.

"It's all about money," his father had said. "A healthy cash reserve is the best protection against financial ruin. Money don't just increase your net worth, but helps you help others — your family, friends and everybody. You'll hear people say that money won't bring happiness, but it's brought more happiness than poverty. Money means a warm home and healthy children, a good education and everything else."

Leroy turned right off the Harrow Road, down the Grove, the sweet sound of soul oozing from the car stereo. He patted the wad of banknotes in his money belt reassuringly. Those boyhood lectures from his father on success in life had stuck with him. With that £1,000 he had saved during his half year at Mickey

Dee's, he had pulled off his first business deal by flying to New York cheap and buying a large stock of black interest T-shirts and baseball caps, all of which sold quickly at that year's carnival, doubling his profits. A few years down the line now and he saw West London as a boomtown ripe for someone like him with a head full of ideas to reap a fabulous harvest. Even though life for his father had not been a crystal stair and he had lost his home, Leroy would still aim for the stars. He had been through failure and frustration, times when money didn't flow too easily if at all, times when the creative juices weren't flowing and times when he felt totally out of touch from the rest of humanity. But it had never once crossed his mind to jack it all in. When he first started out in business he knew where he wanted to go and what he had to do to get there. He had that vivid picture in his mind of his goals and would simply go about the task of achieving them one by one, determined to be the best in whatever he chose to do.

He eased the car forward down the Grove, heading for his office in Terence Yard. Remembering Sharon's message he pulled out his mobile and touched the redial button.

"Hello, Matthew Percy speaking."

"Yaow! This is Leroy... I got a message that someone was looking for me?"

"Leroy Massop? Yes, I've got a message for you from a mutual 'friend' of ours..."

"What you talking about, man, I haven't got all day."

"I can't give you details over the phone... Let's just say a beautiful woman with a lot of influence would like to meet you again to see how she can help the Westview

Youth Project..."

Leroy guessed what Matthew was hinting at.

"Oh you mean the Princess, why didn't you just say so?"

The voice at the other end of the line coughed nervously.

"Please, be careful what you say on the phone... you never know who's listening and it's a matter of national security that we use the utmost discretion."

Leroy said fair enough. He listened keenly as Matthew gave him details of when, where and how he would meet their "mutual friend."

"You do know how to ride a horse, don't you?" Matthew asked.

"Ride? Yeah man, me ride good," Leroy claimed.

"Whoah! Woaaaah!"

Leroy pulled hard on the horse's reins as the stable boy had told him to, but it only seemed to make the horse go faster.

Morning had only just broken over a near-deserted Hyde Park. London had only begun to rise for the new day. But Leroy had arrived at the stables early as Matthew had directed. He was supposed to canter along the Knightsbridge bridle path until he was met by another rider. Instead of cantering however, his mare had bolted through the early morning mist with Leroy hanging on for dear life. It always looked so easy in the movies.

"Whooaaah! Woooah!" he continued yelling at the horse but to no effect. The mare galloped forward as if nothing else mattered. It had left the bridle path and was now racing across the grass. Leroy pulled some more on the reins and the horse went faster. Suddenly, he saw potential disaster looming ahead of him. The mare seemed to be heading straight for the Serpentine — the lake in the middle of the park.

"Ohhh no, ohhhh no!" Leroy cried out. "Whoooaaah! Woooaaaah! Whoah horse, whoah!"

The horse paid no attention but steamed ahead, neighing and panting furiously. Leroy could see disaster just a moment away now, but the mare seemed not to see it. Leroy's heart beat faster and faster, he couldn't stop the horse, he couldn't jump off, he couldn't do anything. The only thing to do was to close his eyes in preparation...."

"Whooooaaah!"

Leroy looked up at the sound of the woman's voice. Beside him in riding dress, the Princess on a thoroughbred horse had gripped hold of Leroy's reins and only just managed to steer the bolted horse to the left of the lake.

Leroy breathed a sigh of relief as his horse slowed down to walking pace.

"Crazy horse," he said to the Princess with a shrug of his shoulders.

The Princess smiled.

"You haven't been riding long have you?"

Leroy admitted that he hadn't.

"It's easy when you know how," she said.

An expert rider herself, the Princess was able to lead Leroy back onto the bridle path, where they rode side by side. There were still very few people in the park, though a short distance behind them Leroy noticed a man on a black horse who seemed to be following them.

"That's Evans my personal bodyguard," the Princess said, motioning backwards with her head.

"What, he follows you wherever you go?"

"I'm afraid so," the Princess replied almost sadly."...Well, not everywhere, there are some places which remain private even for a princess."

Leroy shifted in his saddle to make himself more comfortable. The horse was behaving itself now, and he was getting the hang of it. With the experienced Princess riding beside him his confidence was boosted.

"You know I admire your guts," the Princess said, "not many people would have done what you did at the Youth Centre when you invited me back to meet the youngsters that use it. I was quite impressed."

"Well, you know how it goes..." Leroy replied coyly.

"And then when that young man said that I should have brought jobs with me... it made me think... I haven't been able to put it out of my mind."

"Yeah, things are rough for some of those youths, your Highness. Ain't got no future to look forward to, you know. I don't expect you to know that. I bet the world looks different from Buckingham Palace. Can you tune in to Groove FM from the Palace?"

"Groove FM, what's that?"

"You never hear of Groove? It's the hottest station out there. Ninety-two point two FM — the Groove. It's a pirate of course."

"Pirate? What do you mean?"

"They ain't got a licence, but that's the system, fighting against the youth as usual."

"So this Groove station broadcasts illegally. Really, you shouldn't be telling me this, after all I'm the Princess of Wales. My behaviour has to be impeccable."

The Princess dug her heels into her horse's side and increased the pace to a trot. Leroy followed suit, if not as smoothly but eventually caught up with her.

"That's where you come in though, your Highness. You see, the kids on the Westview Estate wouldn't be broadcasting illegally if they got a licence. They'd get a licence with your support."

The Princess looked across at Leroy riding clumsily beside her. She continued listening.

"If you want to do something practical about those kids' future, this is a good way."

The Princess continued riding, deep in thought. Then suddenly she said:

"I bet a lot of women find you attractive... anyone in particular?"

"What?! Er... no," Leroy answered, with only the slightest hesitation. "I live by myself."

"Really?" the Princess asked interestedly. "Why is that?"

"Well you know how it is, I'm a businessman. I can't find the time for a relationship."

"So you're a businessman. What's the business?"

"Buying and selling, you know the sort of thing, import-export."

Leroy was conscious of trying to impress the Princess. Suddenly he felt overawed by the whole situation; he was actually riding a horse at daybreak in Hyde Park, talking to the Princess of Wales... Leroy turned his head and saw the man on the black horse, still some yards behind but keeping up the same pace.

The Princess glanced at the elegant watch on her wrist.

"It's getting late,"she said, "I'd better be getting back."

Leroy nodded. They were almost at Hyde Park Corner.

"Do you know what I should like?" the Princess said. "I should like you to be my guest at Eglington Hall, my country home. I'll be having a little party there soon. Would you be able to make it?"

"Yeah man," Leroy said casually, his heart pumping fast inside though. This woman liked him it seemed. She was inviting him to a party.

The Princess told him that her secretary would send him an invite and with a wave turned her horse around and galloped off, the bodyguard galloping behind her on the black horse.

CHAPTER 9

The two vehicle convoy made its way out of London, heading West down the M4. The BMW took the lead, its top down, Leroy at the wheel holding a steady 80mph, Lyndon at his side in the front passenger seat, dressed formally in a sequinned black jacket with matching trousers, taking in the revival sounds blasting out of the car speakers. Ragga babes Tracey and Dionne with their short, relaxed hair were at the back, one wearing a micro miniskirt, a revealing bra top and huge gold earrings, the other tiny batty-rider shorts and a corset. They were all looking forward to the party.

Behind the BMW, the white van was struggling to keep pace. It was not only loaded down with oversize speaker boxes and other equipment belonging to Groove International Sound System, but it also carried half a dozen sound boys in regulation ragga suits all ready for the session at Eglington Hall.

Dressed in a baggy matching blue and yellow shorts suit with a hood, Air Darwins and a baseball cap with a red, green and gold motif in the front, Lesley Lyrics looked cool and relaxed.

"Me 'ave 'nuff lyrics, yuh know Rusty," he insisted,

131

"lyrics that entertain all black, white, yellow — everybody."

Still in his teens, Leslie Lyrics was the number one ragga deejay in the country, the MC everybody in west London hoped would go to the Sting clash later in the year and hold his own against the countless Jamaican deejays appearing. Leslie wasn't a deejay who spun records, but one who could chat. He could take the microphone over a steady ragga beat or a ruff jungle beat and fire up the rhythm and entertain with lyrics culled from the darkest corners of his mind. He was a lyrical lexicon whose vocals were imitated in deferential homage, by school kids all over West London. On the street, certain men would swear that Leslie got a lot of youth turning their back on the crack pipe with his hit tune refrain:

*"From the drugs white
The ghetto yout' know dat cyaan right.*

Leslie was hot property and he knew it. So did Rusty.

Daddy Rusty pressed his foot on the gas to keep up with the BMW in front and rubbed his short, well-trimmed beard. He was sweating profusely, insisting on wearing his three-quarter length black coat over a check lumber shirt despite the burning sun. As most people knew, he never took that coat off. He was the driver for Groove International Sounds now, but he had been a successful reggae producer in his heyday. In the seventies when only Jamaican reggae was considered authentic, he created almost single-handedly, a British hybrid — lover's rock. All he did was add strings to lazy

132

reggae rhythms and get a female harmony group in the vein of The Supremes to voice over. The music had been hugely successful, especially amongst younger women who related closely to the 'broken-hearted' lyrics of groups such as Bitter-Sweet and singer Laverne Taylor. His artists' success had made Rusty a wealthy man. He once owned several houses, a couple of slick cars and a converted church in a Harlesden side street which served as his studio. With more money coming in than he knew what to do with, he was preparing himself to retire back home. But then it all came crashing down. Rusty got into an altercation with a musician who felt he had not been paid his dues. The ensuing violent struggle resulted in the musician clinging on to his life with the help of a massive blood transfusion, while Rusty was left with a 'telephone receiver' scar and a three-year sentence for grievous. He lost everything while he was in jail. The Inland Revenue decided to investigate why he had not paid taxes for the previous five years, and ended up helping themselves to all that was left of his wealth. By the time he had come out of jail, lover's rock was dead and a new generation ruled the musical front, with a harder, tougher sound. Nobody remembered Rusty Morgan Productions. Not until Leslie Lyrics offered the veteran producer a second shot at the music business did things once again look promising for Rusty. From the first time he had heard Leslie entertaining his friends with his patter in a local park, Rusty was convinced that the youth had what it took to go all the way to the top. He had been the youngster's manager ever since then, and he also drove the van for Groove International sessions.

At the back of the van perched amongst the speaker boxes, contentedly sharing a spliff, were the rest of the Groove International crew. Magic the engineer, dressed from head to foot in army fatigues, Flabba the selector, who had chosen a denim baggy suit for the trip and Junior and Raymond the security team, in colourful string vests with kerchiefs hanging from the pockets of their baggy blue jeans which were tucked into expensive trainers and with patterned bandanas tied neatly around their heads.

Raymond complained that he suspected Junior of messing up the little air they were sharing at the back of the van.

"When last you really hol' a fresh?" he asked, " 'cause I know you never bathe from morning, man."

"Behave yourself. Your mouth needs to hol' a fresh!" Junior retorted.

Security was an important aspect of any dance and though Raymond and Junior liked to joke, they knew their job was serious business.

Up front in the BMW, Leroy smiled to himself. This was the life. He and his crew were living large. Today they were going to be rubbing shoulders with the rich and famous. Who knew what lay ahead tomorrow?

The invite arrived the week before:

H.R.H. Princess of Wales
cordially requests the company of Mr Leroy Massop Esq.
for the Princess of Wales Horse Trials taking place in the
grounds of Eglington Hall, Worcestershire...

The invite addressed to Leroy Massop, c/o Westview

Youth Project, had a quick note on the back:

"There'll be a great party afterwards, please bring some music - H.R.H."

Leroy didn't have to be asked twice, neither did any of the people from the sound when he asked them to provide the music that the Princess had requested. A day in the country would make a welcome relaxing respite from the urban vibes.

The vehicles continued West down the motorway, stopping only once for refuelling and refreshments at a petrol station. The pump attendant had his mind on other things as he filled the tank of the blue BMW. He had never seen women dressed like Tracey and Dionne before. Glued to the tiny shorts and micro miniskirt his eyes almost popped out of his head and he carried on pumping long after the tank was full.

"Hey bwoy!" Leroy called out, "what the fuck you thinking about! You better clean that petrol off my car, man."

The attendant jumped to attention and went for a rag to clean off the excess petrol.

Junior, Raymond and Magic took the opportunity to stretch their legs, while Flabba preferred to stay in the back of the van, running through the record selection. Those who needed to use the toilets did so and when everyone was gathered again the convoy got back on its way, leaving the pump attendant still dreaming of micro miniskirts and batty riders.

The journey took nearly three hours, driving through some scenic countryside once they had turned off the motorway. Through quiet country roads and sleepy villages they made their way. At one point, woodland was replaced by rolling hills as far as the eye could see and for the next twenty miles of road. On closer inspection, the dotted white flecks on the hillsides turned out to be sheep, a countless number, grazing in the lush green pasture.

"Bloodclaat!" cried Raymond from the back of the van. "Ah Wales dis?"

"More like New Zealand!" Leslie replied from the front.

Rusty smiled a broad smile.

"Enjoy it, man. Get some fresh air in you. Me jus' love dis kinda vibes, y'know."

He continued driving, keeping up easily with Leroy's blue BMW now that they were the only two vehicles on the road — which was looking increasingly like wilderness. The road was to become even smaller, more desolate and more winding and everybody hoped that Lyndon up front in the BMW was reading the road map correctly.

Eventually they saw Eglington Hall — looming majestically in the middle of acres of dreamy hillside.

Built by a renowned eighteenth century architect, Eglington Hall had been in the Princess of Wales' family for three hundred years, bequeathed to the 1st Earl by the crown for his services in war. It was a huge property which boasted a hundred rooms, a dozen other properties on the 1,000 acre estate and a staff of sixty people including full-time gardeners, cooks, maids, farm hands and a game keeper. In fact, so grand was the mansion that it had a long history of playing host to kings and queens of the past. Today, it was to play host to the cream of high society, who had gathered for the annual fundraising Princess of Wales Horse Trials. Hurrah Henrys would mix with Hurrah Henriettas during the day and they would party with one another in the vast hall of the mansion through the night.

Leroy and his crew stared incredulously across at the huge house, none of them saying a word. The two vehicles slowed down as they approached the wide gate. The duty policeman checked Leroy's invite, but refused to let the rest of the crew in without invites. Leroy protested, they had all been invited, these were the artists. The policeman radioed up to the house. He came off the line still suspicious of the youths in the van, but they were to be allowed through. He opened the gate wide and waved the convoy on.

The vehicles drove slowly up the winding gravel driveway. On either side of the drive, deer strolled leisurely and pheasants strutted purposefully with their plumes spread wide, unbothered by the couples and groups of people walking across the lawn. The mansion house ahead revealed itself in all its glory, as the blue BMW and the van got closer. It was a huge building. It was difficult to imagine that just one family lived there. Neither Leroy nor any of his friends had seen this kind of wealth before, wealth which made all their endeavours back in London seem like pocket money. They parked up beside a row of luxury cars, mostly Jags and Mercs and climbed out of their vehicles, everybody stretching after the long journey.

"Yes, fresh country air," Lyndon said, inhaling deeply.

Raymond agreed. Thanks to Junior this was the first taste of fresh air he had had since they left London, he claimed.

Dionne and Tracey said that they needed to visit a bathroom and it was urgent.

Lesley and Rusty were admiring the new series Mercedes parked up beside their van, with the young deejay assuring his manager that when he got his "big break", they would each be driving one just like it.

Leroy simply stood, his head leaned back, trying to figure out how much such a huge mansion was worth.

'Boom!' The first explosion cracked through the air unexpectedly shattering the countryside tranquillity with a deafening sound. It could have been a number of things, a car backfiring, or even thunder. Raymond and Junior exchanged glances. 'Boom! Boom!' The next two explosions were unmistakeable and sent a flock of birds flying skywards in confusion. Gunshots! The sound system posse dived to the ground. Junior and Raymond pulled two fearsome looking 9mm automatics from under their shirts and were ready to use them. The duo had taken the recent precaution of being tooled up when they played a sound session, after death threats from a bad bwoy of a rival sound system.

'Boom! Boom! Boom!' More shots. Crawling along the gravel ground on his stomach, Junior tried to get an angle on where the shots were coming from. He eased himself along between the parked luxury cars slowly, his automatic pointed upwards.

"I say... no need for all that."

Junior looked up. The upper class voice belonged to the pale-faced man now coming towards him from the main entrance of the mansion, with a glass of champagne in one hand and a cigarette in the other.

"There's a hunting party shooting game over in the woods."

Junior's eyes followed the direction in which the man was pointing and made out the clump of trees over in the distance and the group of men in Barber coats all carrying shotguns. Still lying on his belly, the security man turned back to his friends and gave the all clear signal.

"Yeah, everyt'ing cool, seen?"

"Yeah man...!" the upper class man said in a mock Caribbean accent, "cool runnings, man, everything's irie."

The crew rose to their feet slowly. Leroy recognised Matthew immediately and hailed him up. Tracey was still desperate to go to the ladies room while Dionne was now complaining about laddering her tights, but apart from that, everyone saw the funny side. Junior and Raymond tucked their guns discreetly into the back of their waist belts.

"So you must be Leroy," said an upper class woman dressed in a pastel-coloured floral dress.

Lyndon shook his head and pointed to Leroy.

"I'm Lady Jane Frobisher, the Princess' cousin, she said with a flash of her cobalt-blue eyes. I'm so glad you could make it. I see you've already met Matthew..."

The upper class man raised his glass in appreciation and downed the rest of the champagne in one gulp.

For no reason other than that he felt he ought to, Leroy took Lady Jane's hand and kissed it. If his life needed any glamour, this was his opportunity. Her smile in response revealed an inner self-confidence, she wasn't at all phased by the black man in front of her.

Lady Jane led the way into the mansion, where a number of guests were already gathered, drinking champagne and chatting. In the huge entrance hall all heads turned at the sight of the West London 'raggamuffins' striding in coolly. Two waiters coming from opposite directions, each carrying a silver tray laden with filled glasses of champagne, collided in the centre of the hall, their eyes locked in amazement at the two scantily clad ragga babes. Leroy and his crew had already livened up the party and they hadn't even started pumping up the volume.

Lady Jane explained that the Princess would be down later. They weren't expecting Leroy to come with an entire mobile discotheque. The invite said 'bring some music', but the Princess had only meant a few records. It didn't matter though, Lady Jane insisted, now that they were here she was sure they were going to have a great party later. With Matthew still in tow and still drinking champagne, Lady Jane took her guests on a quick tour of Eglington Hall, which had been passed on to the Princess' brother after her father — the 8th Earl — died the previous year. She took them through the drawing room, the library and the picture gallery with portraits in oil by great masters.

"That's my great-great grandfather who was married to the Princess' great-great grandmother, who is also Lady Jane's great-great grandmother," Matthew was explaining to Tracey. They both stood back and admired the oil painting. Everybody else was smirking at the way Matthew talked, but Tracey seemed to be interested, especially when she discovered that he was going to become a Duke as soon as his father was dead. "Oh yes, I love reggae, and I just love Jamaica. I always try and spend at least a week there every winter. It's really cool runnings," Matthew told Tracey.

Leroy's crew followed Lady Jane through to the magnificent state rooms and library, still raising eyebrows amongst the guests and servants alike wherever they went. There was already an excited buzz at the mansion before they arrived, but now it was audible.

Everybody seemed to be pointing towards the newly-arrived black guests and whispering with alarmed looks on their faces. Leroy and his friends weren't phazed though and simply swaggered their hips even more as they toured the mansion.

The tour ended in the magnificent gardens at the back of the house. There were even more guests out there, drinking champagne and relaxing and watching from a distance, the horse trials which were taking place in the field beyond — where a huge marquee had been set up to the side of the show jumping course.

"Yush! Yush!" Flabba called out, beckoning one of the wine waiters who came over with a silver tray laden with filled champagne glasses. Flabba took hold of a couple and sent the man on his way.

"Yeah," I could get used to this kinda living," the Groove selector declared.

"I'm with you there," Raymond said.

"That makes three of us," concluded Junior.

More eyebrows were raised when Leroy's people made their way down to the field to watch the show jumping. It was to be an annual event and had attracted some fine amateur horsemen and women.

While his friends were looking for a good vantage point to watch the show jumping, Leroy stayed up at the mansion, exploring as much of Eglington Hall as he had access to and dreaming about the day when he would own a place like this. It wasn't impossible, he decided. It might take another ten or twenty years, but he had decided that a house like that was something he had to have.

Leroy wanted the best in life. Mediocrity was in his view tantamount to failure. He didn't intend to be one of those people who wait for things to happen to them and therefore never really learn the rules in this game of life. He knew the rules as far as the black community were concerned, but not the rules that enabled the upper class to amass so much wealth. This was his chance to learn. The richest reward awaited the man who played the game of life well. Those who like Leroy, graduated from the university of life usually ended up successful. Now that he had seen what real wealth was about he was no longer content with being a millionaire, his goal would now be to be Britain's first black billionaire, he decided.

Down by the show jumping, Leroy's crew were causing a stir. They were in high spirits and having a good time, cheering the show jumpers on boisterously. This in contrast to the subdued applause from the other spectators whenever a horse cleared a fence.

Rusty started running a little book amongst their crew, taking side bets as to which horses would clear the fences with no faults. Leslie Lyrics ended up owing his manager twenty pounds before he called it quits.

Matthew — who was still with them and still impressing on Tracey — placed a fifty pound bet with Rusty and won. The veteran producer reluctantly paid up and ended up twenty pounds down on when he had started.

Lyndon put it down to jungle fever, but he wasn't surprised that the presence of a group of black men should attract the attention of even the most upper crust of white women at the horse trials. After all, their appearance had added flavour to the occasion, an exotic flavour and when he looked around at the other spectators, he couldn't see any others who looked as interesting, as colourful and as relaxed as his crew. He had noticed the group of sloaney-looking women dressed smartly but sensibly in Burberry's and wellington boots, admiring them almost as soon as they had arrived — one especially who Lyndon noticed giving him the eye coyly. It didn't take him long to make his move and a moment later he was there in the middle of the group, charming them with lyrics. In a moment, Rusty had joined him, followed by Leslie and Magic.

"But you've got to admit, if you had more Jamaicans riding horses, they would clean up out here," Lyndon teased the woman he was chatting up. Lesley agreed with him and so did Rusty and Magic.

"Definitely," Leslie said.

The woman, who introduced herself as Vanessa, giggled.

"Everything we Jamaicans do we succeed in," Rusty added. "Whatever sport. Look how many Jamaican world champion boxers there's been, even if they fly under a flag of convenience... Mike McCallum, Lloyd Honeyghan, Chris Eubanks, Lennox Lewis. And then there's the world champion runners like Linford Christie and Merlene Ottey. Then look at football... Jamaican players run t'ings in the Premier League right now, you know."

"And anyways, there is a Jamaican show jumper you know," Lyndon added. "You know that guy with the dreadlocks you see on TV, wha' him name, Skeets?"

"Him nah Jamaican," Rusty informed, "Him is Bajan or sump'n."

"Well that explains why he's not the best already then, don't it?"

"Is there anything Jamaican men aren't best at?" Vanessa's friend asked, amused by the boasting.

Each one of the men put their hands to their chins pondering but they all had to admit that they couldn't think of anything.

"You ever have a Jamaican man?" Rusty asked one of the women pointedly.

The woman blushed and looked away. Rusty felt no way.

"You see a Jamaican man can make love all twenty-four hours, forty-eight hours and still going strong," he said confidently.

"How yah mean, man?" Flabba enquired. "Still going strong after a week more like."

Vanessa and her friends were laughing away with Lyndon and the others as a stiff-looking white guy took his turn around the show jumping course, dressed in the regulation red jacket, white breeches and black safety helmet. He had almost completed the course without a single fault and now with only three obstacles to complete, the spectators cheered as he completed another fence without a fault. As he swung his horse around to approach the penultimate fence, he caught sight of Lyndon patting Vanessa playfully on the behind. His eyes fixed upon them, a look of astonishment on his face. Without the command to jump, the horse wasn't going anywhere and screeched to a halt just inches from the triple fence. The jockey didn't stand a chance. He went flying over the mane of the horse and landed with a thud on the other side of the obstacle.

The Groove posse witnessed the whole thing along with everybody else and roared with laughter at the sight of the jockey, his tunic covered in horse shit, struggling to his feet in a daze. Victory in the tournament having eluded him, he cursed loudly and made his way off the course.

Lyndon was whispering sweet nothings into Vanessa's ear when the thrown jockey marched up, a trio of fellow jockeys at his side.

"I say Vanessa," the jockey asked the woman, "are these chaps troubling you?"

Vanessa looked up, brushing Lyndon aside for a moment.

"Actually no, Nigel. These men aren't troubling us at all. They're very charming as a matter of fact. You're the one who's troubling us." She turned up her nose at him and gave him a 'mind your own business' look.

Neither Nigel nor his other upper class friends were too happy about seeing the women they had arrived with enjoying themselves and being so well-entertained by these black men.

"Look Vanessa, perhaps we ought to go and have a

chat," Nigel said awkwardly.

"No, you go off with the other boys," Vanessa dismissed him, "I'm sure you fellows have got lots of rugby to talk about."

Lyndon shook his head, smiling and gave the horseman a pitiful look. Nigel was irate, but there wasn't much he could do. He turned to his friends and they each shrugged their shoulders and sauntered off reluctantly. Before he turned to go, Nigel gave Leroy a threatening look. This wasn't over.

The rest of the day unfolded with no major surprises. The winner of the tournament was announced by early evening and people started making their way off the grounds only to return refreshed a few hours later for the promised party at the hall. Leroy had spent most of the day introducing himself to as many people as he could. All the guests at the mansion seemed to be Lords or Ladies, even though some were quite young. It was the perfect opportunity for him to make some contacts.

"Yeah King Lee Enterprises," he told a group of men discussing insider trading, in the landscaped garden behind the mansion house. He handed each of them his business card.

"Leroy Massop... pleased to meet you, managing director of King Lee export and import — international... All kinds of projects from a safety pin to a diamond ring. No order too large, no order too small."

Leroy shook as many people's hands as he could.

Later that evening as the party was under way in the huge entrance hall to the mansion, the Princess finally appeared for the first time that day. There must have been about five hundred guests there, dancing and sitting and chatting, but as soon as the Princess appeared, everybody stopped what they were doing, stood up and applauded. Leroy watched from the side, expecting her to come over and say 'hi'. But she didn't seem to notice him. Instead, surrounded by her ladies-in-waiting, she seemed to be enjoying herself dancing to the sound that had been set up. The sound, operated by a balding white deejay with a long black pony tail was really just an ordinary discotheque, playing Top 40 and club music. The young guests at the hall, all of whom were now in formal evening attire, seemed to be enjoying the music. All except the posse of black youths seated around a couple of tables who had come up from London.

Rusty laughed as he observed the revellers dancing to the simple dance beat.

"Watching white people dance is one of my favourite pastimes," he told Leslie.

The youth agreed, that was always entertaining.

"I think this is kinda boring..." Dionne countered. Unlike Tracey she wasn't impressed by a party filled with Lords and Dukes. When are we supposed to be setting up?" she asked Rusty.

The older man looked at his watch.

"Cho', dis bwoy ah work overtime," he cursed the deejay. "Yuh ready fe tek over?" he asked Leslie who was sitting beside him.

The youth nodded.

"Every time."

The two got up, followed by Magic, Raymond and Junior. They got behind the turntables. To the deejays astonishment, they simply pulled the earphones from his head and pushed him aside.

"Coffee break," Rusty told him with a shrug.

Magic pulled up the needle on the record and switched the white deejay's double turntable with their more compact single turntable. Raymond and Junior didn't need to be told what to do. They immediately began pulling down the deejay's speakers, which were sitting on top of their own enormous Groove International boxes. Leslie took the microphone:

"Now all nice and decent people hear dis —
Now dis is a takeover by the one Groove International Sound, outta Harlesden on the West London side ah t'ings
Now we come to make you feel the bass
Wine up your waist
And get a taste
Of a ruffneck poet, comin' from the black race.
Now ease my selector, come down different..."

Magic maxed up the volume, dropped the needle on the twelve inch vinyl on cue and with an explosion of simulated automatic gunfire, a ragga cut of Slim Smith's *My Conversation* exploded through the speakers.

Groove International's amp box was a hundred times more powerful than a domestic stereo, which gave them the ability to amplify the bass until it sounded like the world's biggest drum. You could feel it in your feet, your ankle bones, your thigh bones. The aristocrats had never heard anything so deafening. It was unbelievable, unbearable, 'Oh my God!" somebody cried.

The guests ran out through the main entrance door into the night outside, ears covered, trying to get as far away from the noise as possible, all except Leroy and his crew who were enjoying it and the Princess who was dancing beside them. Dionne and Tracey had thrown away any inhibitions however and were now performing the 'dutty rub up' with Junior and Raymond in that x-rated way. Rusty who was also on the dancefloor, his fingers cocked in the air like a gun, smiled when he saw the girls dancing. It was nice but he had seen better back in the early seventies when he knew girls who could give some 'dutty rub up' worse than the ragga girls were doing nowadays. This generation were just doing it a bit more pronounced, that was all.

When the other women guests saw the Princess enjoying herself, they cautiously stepped back in, tapping their feet awkwardly to the music and moving closer and closer to Leroy's crew on the dancefloor. Finally, their men joined them on the dancefloor, not wanting to be outdone, but making sure that they kept their eyes tight on their women, or even better kept their arms tight around their women's waists.

"Groove International
The number one sound inna de area
An' if ah bwoy wan' tes'
Come tes' we..."

Leslie was in fine form and soon got the party jumping.

"So you don't remember me?" Leroy asked, trying not to shout over the music, which meant that he had to get very close.

The Princess looked up at him and smiled. Leroy

turned his head for her to speak into his ear.

"It's Leroy isn't it? Of course I do."

She was an alright dancer, Leroy decided, at least she was better than all the other aristocrats around them who were moving too fast to the music. He preferred skanking it easy so that he could talk to the Princess.

"Oh, this is wonderful," the Princess said, tossing her head back casually, really enjoying herself.

"One good thing about reggae, when it hits you, you feel no pain."

"Now where have I heard that before?" the Princess wondered aloud.

"Bob Marley," Leroy admitted, "the reggae king."

"Of course, that's right. Bob Marley, he's my favourite, oh isn't he wonderful?"

They danced together for a while, before the Princess decided that she needed to step out for some fresh air. That was alright for Leroy; they had had a dance and he knew that just one dance could get her asking for more. Like a gentleman, he said that he would accompany her. They stepped out together into the garden, neither noticing the perplexed glances of the other guests.

Outside, it was still warm and the full moon above illuminated the landscaped garden. There were several couples strolling amongst the rhododendron, arm in arm. Other guests chatted casually while sipping more and more champagne, getting more and more drunk.

The ragga and the royal strolled casually, chatting aimlessly. There were so many things for them to talk about because they lived such separate lives and the Princess was as fascinated about what Leroy did as he was to hear about what she did.

"My area is ruff," Leroy began, wanting to impress her "It's like Vietnam down there — the hardest of the hardest survives."

"West London's not really like that," the Princess stated.

"Yeah man, it is. When was the last time you were down in Harlesden? Okay you have some man who's cool, but a next man is tense — that's when it gets rough. But I love it still."

The Princess admired Leroy's bejeweled fingers. He smiled and said, "Let's talk about you."

"I am not what I am," the Princess said, tossing her head back with an enigmatic smile.

Leroy smiled back without knowing exactly what she meant.

"I just mean I'm not what I want to be. I want to be an ordinary person again. That's who I am inside, but since I married the Prince of Wales I haven't been allowed to be myself"

"Do you dream?" Leroy asked.

"Of course I do..."

"What do you dream about?"

"Oh, all sorts of things... you can't expect me to stand here and tell you my dreams, that's a personal thing.

"Carry on," Leroy insisted.

"Well... I dreamt about meeting you."

At that moment there was a stern cough behind them. They both spun around and stood face-to-face with Evans, the Princess' bodyguard. His face looked mean. He had obviously been eavesdropping on their conversation.

"What the ...?!" Leroy began.

"It's alright," the Princess said. "This is the price I have to pay for being a royal. He's my bodyguard. Evans, you don't need to be shadowing me. This is a private party, nothing's going to happen to me here."

"Just doing my job, your highness," Evans said.

"That's alright, but I'd like to have a private conversation with this gentleman, if you don't mind."

The bodyguard didn't like it. He grunted before turning to join the rest of the party in the house.

Leroy smiled, this Princess was fine and he could see she was more than ready to make a move with him.

Everybody agreed that it had been a great party. Things were still lively into the early morning, nobody seemed to want to call it a night. The champagne was still flowing strong and the guests were becoming even more drunk. One drunk woman walked straight up to Rusty, who was skanking it easy on the dancefloor and demanded a "fuck"! He couldn't believe what he heard and at first pretended to be picking up a drink or something. Then the woman insisted that he accompany her outside for a breath of fresh air.

"Well watcha now," Rusty replied, "my people dem suppose to come fe me, y'know."

But the woman insisted.

Rusty finally agreed, not wanting her to think he was racist and walked out of the mansion with her. Once outside, the woman — who was quite unsteady on her feet — suddenly demanded that Rusty kiss her.

"Come on, give me a kiss —now!"

The woman grabbed him and dived into his half-open mouth with her tongue, hiccoughing all the time.

"Hey nigger!!!"

The shout behind Rusty's ear was so loud that he jumped back, pushing the woman away. To his left, three of the upper class guys from the show jumping earlier in the day, were making their way towards him. Almost instinctively, Rusty picked up an empty champagne bottle balanced on a low wall and broke it in half. The three white boys stopped dead in their tracks, their eyes frozen on the jagged edge of the bottle pointing in their direction. From the look in Rusty's eyes they could see that he wouldn't hesitate to use it.

"Who the bumbaclaat you calling 'nigger'?! So yuh waan come tes' me? Come tes', nuh!"

"Rebecca, you slut..!!" one of the youths called out to the unsober woman.

If Rusty's concentration wasn't on the three youths, he might have seen Evans, move up stealthily on his blind side. He didn't see the Sergeant's foot kick the broken bottle out of his hand either. In the next swift movement, Evans had handcuffed Rusty's hands behind his back. He flashed his ID in Rusty's face and said, "Police."

"Was this the gentleman who stole your wallet, sir?" Evans turned to the three men, who were as surprised as Rusty was by the turn of events.

"Yes, that's him," said Nigel after a brief hesitation.

"Alright, sir," Evans addressed Rusty, "come with me, you'll be spending the night at the station until it's all cleared up. Your sort aren't wanted around here."

Rusty protested his innocence, but to no avail. Evans took him around to the front side of the mansion where his black Rover was waiting to ferry Rusty to the local police station.

"Wicked place you've got here," Leroy said. "Boy, you don't know how lucky you are."

"Oh yes I do," said the Princess mysteriously, "I'm able to go out and meet charming men like you and invite them back to any of my homes and they are always suitably impressed. Yes, I suppose I am very lucky in some respects."

Leroy smiled. He liked women who came straight to the point.

They sipped at their coffees, chatting away. Leroy wasn't a novice in this game; he knew he was in with a chance. He had read up some books on the royal family to do some research on the Princess and he knew that she was a bit of a raver.

They talked until they were both tired.

"I don't know what it is..." the Princess whispered in Leroy's ear, "you're so nice, so nice."

Leroy had to think quickly. He was sitting on a sofa in the Princess' private apartment upstairs in Eglington Hall and she had made a half pass to him, that was half a chance he had to take.

"So, do you want me to stay the night?" he asked eventually.

"So," she echoed, "do you want to stay the night?"

Leroy's smile left no doubt as to the answer. He could think of nothing better. His heart pumped away furiously, trying to jump out of his mouth. This was it, he was going to make it. It was like a dream. Was this all really happening to him? Was he really sitting in the Princess' of Wales's private apartment? Somehow he managed to play it cool.

"Well, I'm ready to go to bed straight away," he said no longer beating about the bush.

The Princess got up and took Leroy's hand, leading him into the adjoining master bedroom, which was huge and with a king size four-poster bed in the middle.

"Make yourself comfortable, I'll just be a minute," she said, pausing long enough before disappearing into the en suite bathroom to say with a smile: "You're going to be my black prince tonight."

"Yes!" Leroy half-shouted, punching his fist in the air triumphantly. This was definitely a result, not just a result, but THE result. Nobody was going to believe that he had got off with the future Queen of England. All he could think about was the great business potential any liaison with the Princess would bring.

He pulled his shirt off his back as fast as he could, losing a couple of buttons in the process, then it was off with his shoes and trousers as fast as he could, stumbling slightly with them around his ankles. He hopped on one foot onto the bed and then pulled them off all the way. He lay there naked on the perfumed duvet, still unable to believe his good fortune. This was going to mean that Groove was definitely going to get a radio licence. He had the whole world in his hands. The future Queen of England was his mistress, he a black man... He could change the course of history. In years to come there could be a real black Queen on the throne all because of him. Whichever way he played it, he would end up rich. Then a thought interrupted his euphoria: maybe she only wanted him for a one night stand, maybe she only wanted a bit of rough on the side? No matter, as long as he was getting something out of it. He lay on his back, looking up at the ceiling, his fingers wandering over the soft silk sheets to the walnut headboard... It felt like a button. Leroy pressed it instinctively for no other reason than because it was on the headboard. Within seconds, Evans the bodyguard had burst into the room with two uniformed officers all with their pistols drawn.

"Get down,!" Evans yelled, waving the gun in Leroy's face. "On your knees, hands above your head...!!"

"Just cool it!" Leroy was shouting. "Just cool it..."

"Shut up! Make a move and I'll blow your head off."

Still naked, Leroy complied, the guy seemed serious. Evans handcuffed Leroy's hands then dragged him to his feet and pushed him forward towards the bedroom door.

"Hey man," Leroy was protesting, "the Princess is waiting for me, you know..."

Evans pushed him forward roughly.

"Sure, sure," the detective said, "all I know is that her Highness' panic distress button went off and you were trespassing in her room. Do you think anyone's going to believe that the future Queen of England invited some naked sambo into her room?"

With another shove, Leroy stumbled out of the Princess' private apartments.

CHAPTER 10

"Let me tell you something about Patsy," the heavily-pregnant Donna said as she and Leroy sat eating Sunday brunch together on the rooftop patio of the Negril Cafe on Portobello Road, "she needs more loving than you've been giving her. You were crazy not devoting all your time to her when she was around. No disrespect, Leroy, but you were stupid. A nice, intelligent, attractive girl like Patsy was the best woman you were going to find. Now you've lost her to this American guy, that's why she keeps flying off to New York to see him."

For a moment, Leroy thought about the weekend before when he had got to see how the other half live. He had spent the night in the only cell at the tiny local police station. Rusty was also in there. They were later joined by Flabba, Magic and Leslie — all threatened with trumped up robbery and theft charges. Raymond and Junior were the last to be brought in. Fortunately when they had seen the police rounding up their crew, the security team had managed to avoid Evans, the Princess' private bodyguard, long enough to hide their weapons. They might yet be sitting huddled together in the cell, if it wasn't for Tracey and Dionne's quick thinking. They got Matthew to send a lawyer down to the station who managed to get them out without even being charged. The whole affair pissed Leroy off no end, but he had got such a taste for the high life that he was looking for one more opportunity.

"Just tell me straight, Donna, have I got any chance of getting Patsy back? I need her back."

Donna smiled. Leroy was dependent on her now, because Patsy refused to speak to him, refused to answer her door to him, refused to take his calls. Leroy needed her to relay his woman's feelings. It was ironic.

"It seems like you love her very much but yet you didn't show that in the ways she needed to see it. How could your woman ever feel confident about your relationship, if after she's been abroad working for two weeks she comes home and you don't even have time to see her, because of all your precious money-making schemes? Well now another man wants to take your place in her affections. That will teach you in future when you're running off to greener pastures, that yours may be green enough already, at least the person who's busy working on it thinks so."

Leroy took a bite of his croissant and washed it down with a sip of mineral water. This was going to take a long time. He could tell that Donna intended to milk his dilemma for all it was worth, but he needed her more than she needed him. He couldn't explain why he didn't want to lose Patsy, but right now he didn't mind taking all the distress she was prepared to dish out, if it only meant that she would give their relationship another chance.

"So how does this yank treat her better than I used to

do?"

Donna smiled again. She had seen Patsy just the other day and her friend had talked at length about how romantic and considerate J.R. Reynolds was.

"Well, for example, wherever she flies to in the world, he always calls her to make sure she's arrived okay, and to see how she's doing. Now you never used to do that, did you? How could you have thrown away her love for you so easily, Leroy? Patsy would have done anything for you. Even a blind man can see that she is worth as much love as you've got to give her."

Donna didn't need to tell him, Leroy could feel his mistake. Patsy hadn't needed to leave him for him to appreciate that he would never find a better romance.

"What else did she say?"

Donna continued.

"She says that she feels close to J.R because he always 'touches' her in a way that you never did."

"Oh come off it," Leroy protested, "she can't say I didn't touch her, how can you make love without touching, how can you kiss without touching, how can you sleep in the same bed without touching? That is just not true."

"Patsy doesn't mean touching her with your hand, but a much more intimate 'touch', touching her soul, her spirit. You can touch your partner with your eyes, you know. You've heard of the 'look of love' haven't you? Now don't you think it would touch your woman in her soul if you gave her that look every now and then? And you can touch her with words. It doesn't have to be any fancy words, just 'I love you' every now and then. Patsy says she never gets tired of hearing J.R. say, 'I love you'.

And she never has to ask him to hug her, or kiss her or love her, or go out with her. He does all those things without being asked and that touches her."

Leroy shifted uneasily in his seat. It was painful to hear from a third party why some yank had succeeded in pulling his woman. He could understand Patsy's feelings and knew all about her pride. She had every right to leave him, he just wished she would give him another chance. He wondered what the yank was now saying to his woman that he should have said. Why had he always held back when she needed a gentle touch?

"Now at least you'll know what life is about after this," Donna said philosophically as she polished off the remains of the omelette on her plate. "Put it down to experience, that's the name everyone gives to their mistakes. Your mistake was that you thought you could serve two masters — your woman and money. That just can't work, choose one or the other. You can't be a slave to money and expect to fulfil the needs of your woman at the same time, that's impossible. Put it this way, you can live to become bankrupt several times over and bounce back each time by making fortunes several times over; your house can burn down and you can replace it, but you're never going to be able to replace a woman like Patsy."

Leroy couldn't accept that his efforts to become wealthy could have negative effects on his relationship. Ever since he was young he had dreamed of becoming wealthy and finding a woman just like Patsy to share that wealth with. He insisted that he was building for the future of their relationship.

"But everything that is really worthwhile in life

160

comes free, like our minds, our souls, dreams, ambitions, intelligence and love. That's all Patsy wanted from you; she didn't care if you never had a penny, as long as you could give her your love. Really give her your love."

Donna looked at her watch and realised that she had to go in a hurry.

"I'll give you a call when I hear any more from Patsy," she said.

"So tell me, is there any point in my trying to get her back or is it too late?"

"It's never too late, y'know, Leroy."

"Alright then what do I do now, how do I get her back?"

Donna stood up, collecting her things together.

"If you really want her back, why not change your life completely, to prove to her how serious you are? Why not just turn your back on all your business deals, why not give your BMW away to a friend and give all your money to charity? Maybe then she'll believe that you value her more than you value silver and gold."

Leroy left enough money to cover the bill, and got up to leave also. Donna must have been joking, she knew that he wasn't about to abandon everything he had spent the last few years building up. That was totally out of the question.

Leroy escorted Donna through the busy Sunday market down to her car and watched her drive away before heading to his vehicle parked over in Powis Square.

"Hey Leroy!"

Leroy spun around, he recognised that upper class

accent. It was Matthew, with a busty black woman on his arm.

"Enough respect!" the white man said, offering his fist for Leroy to touch. Leroy considered how much more black culture Matthew had picked up in the week since the weekend at Eglington Hall. He had suddenly got a taste for black women, since his brief fling with Tracey and would now frequently hang out around the All Saints Road area.

"You know, I've been meaning to get hold of you," Matthew began cheerfully. "Got a message from you know who," he continued with an exaggerated wink of his eye, "and she would like to see you again... oh by the way, this is Cynthia."

Leroy nodded at the big busted woman.

"So how can I contact 'you know who'?" Leroy mimicked.

"I can tell you where she's going to be tomorrow evening."

Matthew pulled out a pen and quickly scribbled down an address.

"It's a really well known restaurant in Knightsbridge called Paulo's. You can't miss it."

"Why don't you just give me her phone number?"

"No that' not a very good idea. All her phones are tapped. MI6 you know. So how have things been old chap? Great session at Eglington. Thoroughly enjoyed myself."

At that moment a vision in canary yellow robes crossed the road over to them. Bongo Zeb was a well-known character in the Portobello Road area where he had featured for as long as people could remember, quoting passages from the Bible loudly in an apocalyptic voice. Without uttering a word, the old rastaman handed Matthew a dog-eared postcard. Puzzled, the white man looked down at the postcard which depicted a grey-haired black man looking wise, regal and majestic beside the caption "What colour is God?"

Matthew stared at the card, not knowing what this was all about. He didn't know whether he was expected to answer the question, or whether he should go about his business in a hurry. He handed the card back with a puzzled look on his face and shrugged his shoulders.

"Yuh see wha' me ah show you," Bongo Zeb suddenly turned to Leroy, rejoicing, "Everyt'ing works in opposites, 'hot' and 'cold', 'day' and 'night', 'sun' and 'moon', 'heavy' and 'light', 'black' and 'white'... So 'black' is the opposite of 'white', God is black, therefore the devil is white... Death to the devil!"

At which point the rasta man raised his heavy African staff high above his head waving it in Matthew's direction. The upper class man didn't need another hint, but hot-stepped away, dragging his girl behind him.

Leroy also decided to step away quietly and leave the old man still ranting on about the devil.

He couldn't believe what had been going on. No, he owed it to the honour of his country to make sure that whatever the Princess and the ragga guy were planning with each other, he would stay just a short distance away, always in full eye contact, making sure her interests were fully protected. The Princess' bodyguard drove his Rover steadily down the motorway... he was going at 100 miles per hour, but he had special dispensation for that. No police would flag him down. Which was just as well, because he always had to shoot up and down the country and sometimes breaking the law was the only way he could perform his royal duties expertly. He knew where his duties lay, it was with the crown, with the royal family and with the United Kingdom. He was one of those dependable officers who the crown always knew that they could rely on to perform any mission however sensitive, and now he had another duty to perform. He was proud of the way he was perceived inside the Force and by the royal family. Especially the Princess who he had come to see as a personal friend. They had been close, sometimes too close, and like everybody else he found her beautiful at close quarters. If only... but no it was impossible, his rank would never allow it. He was a mere mortal, a member of the citizen classes and his was the duty of always looking up to the royal family and being a servant. He couldn't, wouldn't presume to express his feelings for the Princess... But what he didn't like was this black guy coming on strong. He didn't know what their relationship was, but the black guy had been spending one too many nights with the Princess in Evans' view. He refused to believe that the Princess would actually sleep with the guy. He recognised Leroy's type. He was sure that Leroy Massop had a criminal record and he had put a call through to his friends at Scotland Yard. They had run his name and birth date up on their computers, but hadn't come up with anything.

"Not even a charge of possession?" the detective had

asked hopefully.

The answer was negative. Leroy Massop it seemed, was clean.

He drove into a slip road and pulled over. After a few minutes a racing green Aston Martin Volante pulled up beside him... The dark window was wound down and the face of the Prince of Wales peered across on the other side.

"So," the Prince said, "what have you got for me?"

The detective handed over a manila envelope. The Prince opened it, pulling out a series of photographs of his wife accompanied by Leroy. There were pictures from their early morning ride in Regent's Park and photographs from the weekend in the countryside.

The Prince shook his head slowly.

"So what can you tell me about this fellow?" he asked.

"No record sir, it's been difficult finding out a lot of information, but we're working on it."

"You'll have to speed it up," the Prince insisted. "Make sure you stop him from seeing her."

"Sir, you know your estranged wife is a very determined woman. She decides what she wants to do."

"Yes, the Prince said after a long pause. "She's always been like that. But I can't believe that she is more determined than the entire British secret service... You know what it would mean to the Crown if this thing continued. It would be extremely embarrassing. Best try and cover it up as much as possible, and keep working on hindering him. Keep me in touch."

With that the Prince pressed a button and his window wound up with an automatic whir. The Aston Martin roared away. The detective sighed and drove away.

CHAPTER 11

Leroy awoke early Monday morning. The preset clock radio was silent, Groove FM was still off the air. Shaking the sleep out of his head, he showered then went to the kitchen for some breakfast. He searched in the cupboards to no avail however. He had instant coffee, instant tea, instant milk, instant potatoes, instant rice and much more besides, but no real food. There was no cereal and no juice and he couldn't even make a slice of toast. His was a bachelor larder, for the unprepared man. It was so convenient when he had the key to Patsy's flat, because even though she spent most of her time overseas with her job, her cupboards always seemed to be full of fresh food. And then when she flew home, there was always the bonus of some real home cooking. Patsy could turn her cooking into one of the highest arts known to man. That all seemed so long ago in the past, but brought vividly to mind when he considered that his luxury two bedroomed maisonette on Oxford Gardens could never be a real home without a woman.

First stop of the day was to Terry's warehouse — a huge lock-up situated under the Westway just off Portobello Green, between a popular music venue and a youth club. The BMW pulled up outside and Leroy climbed out wearing darkers. It was still morning, but the sun was bright.

He squeezed past the steady flow of traders who were both coming and going and stepped into the warehouse that was overspilling with goods of every shape, size and texture. Though Terry was a few years older than Leroy, they had known each other since their secondary school days. Even then Terry had shown a great knack for the art of making money. When everybody else had a paper round, Terry had three which he completed every morning before school. He also ran the tuck shop at school and in the evenings and weekends he ran his own car valet service, employing a group of school mates to go around with a chamois leather and polish, knocking on people's doors and offering to shine their car for a fee from which Terry took a commission. He always had more money than everyone else as a result, which meant that he had lots of friends — especially girlfriends. Now he was a high roller with his own successful business.

Terry was a wholesaler who dealt in just about everything and made sure that his products moved fast. Because there just wasn't room for dead stock in the warehouse, you could usually pick up good discounts from Terry and he was always open to an offer. For this reason, Terry was hugely successful, providing the raw product for most of West London's street traders and stretching his operations as far away as the Wembley and Southall areas. The fact that Terry was cheaper than any other wholesaler and that his products always seemed to sell fast in the black community, meant that

Leroy could make some change distributing them through his network of street traders, so he was usually in and out of the warehouse a couple of times a week.

Terry was over in the back office simultaneously attending to a customer and speaking frantically on the phone. Leroy tapped the window, Terry turned around and raised his finger up at him — one finger to indicate that he should wait a minute. Leroy pulled out a cigarette and lit it. He had been meaning to give up smoking, it wasn't doing his lungs any good. If he was doing all this hard work to someday become the richest black man in Britain, he wanted to be around to enjoy the fruits of his labour. Maybe four a day wouldn't do much harm...

He puffed slowly on the cigarette. There was a lot of sitting and hanging around in business, but he didn't mind, working for yourself was better than slaving for babylon any day. Finally Terry emerged from his office, shaking the hand of the Asian man who had been sitting in the little Portakabin with him.

"Yeah Leroy... so what you sayin', man?

"Yeah you know how it goes... So how's business...?"

"Oh so-so," said Terry modestly, waving a dismissive hand over the warehouse. "Can't complain, but you know the wonga ain't what it used to be."

'Yeah, yeah', thought Leroy, Terry always complained that the business wasn't doing too good.

"By the way, the filth were down here looking for you this morning."

Leroy raised his eyebrow. The idea of police looking for him was always bad news.

"Yeah a couple of guys, plain clothes, Special

Branch."

'Shit!' Leroy thought, that could only mean one thing... they were checking up on him because they had found him in the Princess of Wales' bedroom.

"What did they ask?"

"Ah you know, the usual thing: how much business you did here, how often you came in, all that sort of thing. To tell you the truth, I wasn't really paying attention, a shipment was coming in at the time."

Leroy shrugged. If the police were sniffing around for something, he would have to make sure that they came out disappointed.

"Yeah," said Terry reverting to the business at hand,"this is what I called you up about..."

He pulled out a bottle of perfume from a box.

"Look at these mate... genuine Chanel perfume... the best. I've got a consignment going really cheap."

"How cheap?"

"I could let you have five hundred bottles at a fiver a bottle."

"A fiver!" Leroy exclaimed suspiciously. "Are you sure that these aren't just some Hong Kong fake? This stuff is expensive, you know."

"Check for yourself."

Terry opened up a bottle and smeared some perfume on Leroy's wrist. Leroy sniffed it. It seemed alright.

"I'll take a sample with me and get back to you tomorrow morning."

"You've got to move fast. This stuff's going to go, believe me. I won't have to lift a finger to shift this lot. You're not going to get a better price anywhere. Do you know how much money you can make selling this stuff out on the street?"

Leroy had already made a mental calculation. He had to admit that it was going to be a lot.

"I don't care, man, I'm gonna get it checked out first. That reminds me that I've got a bone to pick with you..."

"With me?" said Terry innocently.

"Those sneakers man. Who the raas is Mike?"

"Honestly Leroy, that was a misunderstanding. Anyway you've got nothing to complain about, I let you have them for practically next to nothing."

"Practically next to nothing is not good enough. I haven't been able to shift a single one. That means I'm gonna have to give 'em away for nothing, which means I lose out on my 'practically next to nothing' investment. You know I'm not in the business of losing money. Not even next to nothing."

Terry apologised once again and said that he would throw in an extra two dozen bottles of perfume for free and he couldn't say fairer than that. Leroy said he'd get back to him.

Dressed in a dinner jacket Matthew had lent him earlier that afternoon, Leroy casually stepped into the exclusive Paulo's restaurant on the Old Brompton Road. All eyes turned in his direction and the maitre de thought he must be lost. Dinner jacket or no dinner jacket, they seldom had diners with funki dreds.

"Can I help you, sir?" the balding Italian man said.

"Yes, I'm supposed to be meeting a young lady here."

"The table is booked under which name?"

"Er... I don't know who booked it, I'm looking for a

lady... She's a very important Welsh lady...?" Leroy winked his eye exaggeratedly.

"Welsh lady? Do you not have a last name?"

"No I don't, but she's a very important *Welsh* lady," Leroy winked again, this time more determinedly.

The maitre de sighed a sigh of exasperation.

"Alright sir, follow me."

He led the way into the restaurant then waved his hand in a gesture that said 'do you see her here?'

Leroy scanned the restaurant quickly, his eyes darting from one table to the other. But amongst the largely middle-aged business types and their dinner dates, he didn't see the Princess. He scanned quickly again. His eyes suddenly fell on a figure that he recognised sitting alone. The brunette wig had thrown him the first time, but even with her back to him she seemed to fill the restaurant with her presence.

"That's her," he thanked the maitre de, who raised his eyebrow in surprise.

"Leroy," the Princess said, offering him her hand to kiss.

"You alright?"

"Yes, it's really good to see you. You obviously got my message then?"

"Just wait a second..."

Leroy turned and walked towards the maitre de. The short Italian man was observing him suspiciously from a distance.

"You see that woman there?" Leroy pointed in the Princess' direction, "I want to impress her, so I need you to give us the best service you've ever given anyone."

The maitre de, puffed out his chest proudly.

"Yes..." Leroy continued, taking a £50 note out of his wallet, "and here's why."

He flashed the £50 note in front of the maitre de's eyes and then tore it in half. Then he handed one half to the Italian man and pocketed the other half.

"As long as we get the best service, you'll get the other half when we're leaving."

The Italian man smiled a broad smile and assured Leroy that as far as he was concerned he was going to treat him as if he were the King of England.

"Good disguise," Leroy said when he sat back down.

The Princess straightened her wig slightly.

"Do you like it? Nobody recognises me in it. Isn't that incredible? I'm the world's most photographed woman but if I change the colour of my hair from blonde to brunette nobody recognises me."

Leroy looked around suspiciously.

"Where's your detective bodyguard?"

"Oh I managed to give him the slip. I wanted to see you alone. I've given him the slip several times before." She laughed. "The poor man almost has a heart attack every time."

"I don't think he likes me very much."

"Well you can forget about him because he won't be troubling you tonight."

The meal turned out to be really good and the service was fantastic, with the maitre de bending backwards personally, to make sure that the couple were waited on hand and foot and their every need taken care of.

"I'm really enjoying this," the Princess said, "smiling sweetly at Leroy over her wine glass. It's so good to get a chance to just get away from all the pressures of being a member of the royal family and just go out and have fun with one's real friends. Do you know what I mean?"

Leroy said he did.

"So you don't like being a royal, despite all your privileges and all those big houses you get to live in?"

"You get tired of living in big palaces and having everything done for you. You get tired of the endless round of tea parties, cocktail parties, dinners, dances and balls. I yearn so much for the simple life sometimes. If I had never married into the royal family I could have lived a very happy life as an ordinary member of society. But I made my decision and now I have to live with it."

She sounded melancholy. Still, Leroy told her straight what he thought.

"I wouldn't say no to living like that... I wouldn't get tired of it either. Believe me... Yeah, I'd have some serious raves in that palace of yours if it was up to me..."

"But would you want to give up your freedom? Would you like your life to be determined by others? As future Queen of England all my actions are subject to scrutiny. Even my children aren't really mine, they're the property of the state!"

Leroy remembered that the Princess had not only provided her husband with a male heir, she had even provided him with a spare.

"So why aren't you together with the Prince any more?" Leroy asked, recalling all the stories in the papers of a break-up between the royal pair.

"Oh we're always rowing and shouting at each other. Charles never loved me, he only ever regarded me as a suitable person to be the mother of his children. We

173

haven't slept together for years. I can't stand the sight of him and he feels revolted by me."

Leroy couldn't believe what he was hearing. Was she really talking about the marriage that the press had once dubbed 'the love-match of the century'?

"It's all a facade," she continued. "Everything has to be so perfect in royal circles. I hate it, but once you're married into it you can't get away from it. It was a loveless relationship. We're totally different, like chalk and cheese. He's stuffy and boring and he was always unfaithful. For years I had to sit by and watch as my husband had one love affair after another. I eventually accepted the affairs, but I can't accept that he chooses an old bag over spending the night with me, that's too much. And it's my turn to have some fun now."

She winked at Leroy. He had been studying her closely and concluded that despite her position, she was insecure. Even during dinner, she was always checking in the little mirror in her purse and readjusting her hair and make-up, as if she feared losing her looks at any moment.

"Were you ever in love with him?" he asked.

"Yes, whatever 'in love' means. I was young and innocent."

"So if you separate from the Prince of Wales, won't they be able to take your title away from you?"

"Oh they can't do that," she assured him, "because whatever happens in my relationship, I'll always be the mother of the future King of England."

After they had finished the meal and were relaxing with some coffees, the Princess suddenly announced that she had a gift for Leroy. She pulled out a small packet wrapped in decorative paper from her handbag and handed it to him. Embarrassed, Leroy slowly unwrapped it.

"I'm afraid I haven't got anything for you."

"That's alright, Leroy."

Leroy's eyes opened wide as he pulled out a gold and silver clock from the royal jeweller, Asprey. It must have cost her a packet.

"I hope you like it," the Princess said. "I saw this beautiful diamond-studded tie pin and I thought of getting you an Armani suit to go with it, but I didn't know your size. Maybe I could take you shopping for a suit sometime."

Leroy said he'd like that. The Princess smiled, then suddenly a tear fell from her eye, rolling slowly down her cheek.

"What's up?" Leroy asked.

"Oh Leroy, we have to maintain a clandestine relationship. It must never get in the papers that I'm seeing a black man. Despite everything I still have my duty to the country and my children to think about."

Leroy nodded. He didn't mind. He had already assumed that the chances of having the Princess as his woman was completely out of the question. He assured her that he would keep their liaisons confidential.

"You see, I'm tough on the outside, but I'm like marshmallow on the inside," she admitted.

"So tell me," Leroy said with a smirk on his face, "do you royals really have blue blood?"

She laughed.

"Believe it or not, that's not the first time I've been asked that."

They amused each other for a while longer, all the time being treated like royalty by the restaurant's service staff. Leroy found the Princess to be a lot of fun, but she was also confused. 'Maybe that goes with the job', he thought.

The Princess found Leroy to be good company. It crossed her mind that it would have been easier if he were white, 'but then', she thought, 'he wouldn't be black would he?'

"Oh Leroy," she said enthusiastically, "wouldn't it be wonderful to have just one night of passion together?"

Yes, Leroy agreed — few men in the country would pass up a chance to have just one night of passion with the Princess of Wales. He called for the bill. The Princess reminded him that royals didn't carry money: "it's tradition." It was alright, Leroy had enough cash in his money belt to cover everything. On the way out, he gave the Maitre de the second half of the £50 note and the man thanked him profusely.

The Princess and Leroy had parked their separate cars close to each other. They would drive to Leroy's flat in Ladbroke Grove, where they could be more discreet and he would drive her back to her Mercedes early the next morning

They paused outside Paulo's for a second to check their direction. At the same moment the pop of a flashgun exploded in the night air. Both Leroy and Diana were taken by surprise.

"Oh no, this is terrible, this is terrible!" Diana shouted.

Seeing how distraught she was, Leroy walked quickly in the direction of the photographer standing beside his

Harley Davidson motorcycle lining up another shot.

"Give me that film," Leroy demanded, his hand outstretched.

The photographer's face appeared from behind the camera.

"And who the hell are you? Fuck off!"

Leroy would have thumped him there and then, but the Princess had come over to appeal to the photographer's sense of decency.

"I must have that film, please..." she begged, "you don't know what this could do to me... please give it to me... I feel so trapped."

The photographer wasn't budging however. He simply crossed his arms, smiling. Leroy made his way around the other side of the man and kicked the Harley Davidson off its side stand and tilted it just enough to be able to steady it, gripping the handlebars.

"You decide," he told the photographer threateningly.

The photographer simply stared at his gleaming Electra Glide, shocked. He had no doubt that this funki dred would let the bike fall and destroy his pride and joy on which he had laboured for years customising it. The choice was simple, he handed over the film.

As soon as he gave the Princess the film, she stopped her pleading, turned around and left without even thanking the guy. She had got what she wanted and that was all that mattered. Leroy followed her towards the cars.

Detective Sergeant Evans, the Princess' personal bodyguard, had been sitting in the back of the grey

Transit van parked illegally on the opposite side of the road from Paulo's restaurant, for nearly four hours. The Princess often thought she gave him the slip, but as a royalty protection officer it was more than his job was worth to lose her. Even in the restaurant she was in no danger. His men were in there posing as diners and he was confident that nobody could get near her without them knowing.

He had listened in to the Princess' dinner date with this Leroy Massop. He had heard everything, thanks to the sophisticated listening equipment rigged up in the Transit, equipment he had learned to use since bugging the royal family on the current round-the-clock surveillance of all royal calls.

Since arresting Leroy in the Princess' room, he had built a thick file on the black man, including medical records, school records and a list of his friends and associates. He had even got Massop's address and bugged his flat — just in case. If he knew these blacks well, Leroy was bound to slip up at some point. And then Evans would personally throw the book at him. It hadn't been difficult getting that junkie Matthew to give him information about the restaurant date either. For a snort of coke, Matthew was anybody's.

After years of being the Princess' personal bodyguard he had got to know her well. And even though he was a mere commoner, he held a deep passion for her Highness. Duty and the hierarchy of things demanded that this passion remain firmly within his breast pocket however and he had often fantasised about letting her know how he felt and asking if she felt the same way also. It wasn't inconceivable. She had been without physical affection from her husband for some time now, he knew that for a fact, yet she was young and fit, attractive and full of all the natural feelings and desires of a woman her age. Maybe she longed for him to reveal himself...

Either way, there was no way he was going to let the black guy get off with her. That would be unthinkable. In defence of the realm and of his heart's desires he was going to be a law unto himself. He was going to stop Massop taking the Princess to his flat.

He had already radioed through to the local Notting Hill nick and told them that there was a suspected IRA terrorist somewhere in Massop's Oxford Gardens flat. Then he called a contact of his on a national and told him to send a photographer. Evans knew the Princess wouldn't like photographs. But now the pair were driving away in Massop's car and he had to follow them. He climbed into the driver's seat of the Transit and spun the wheel around, pointing the van in the direction of Ladbroke Grove.

The Princess leaned her head back against the leather seat of Leroy's BMW as he spun the car northwards, cruising easy. It was the first time she had been in the Ladbroke Grove area for a long while. But she felt good about it. She relaxed and lost herself in the manic jungle beat coming out of the car stereo, the voice of the deejay screaming out loud:

"We'll take you high, so high so high, so high. We'll pick you up, and take you higher. Cause this one's armed and

extremely dangerous. And wicked and wicked and wicked and rough... Ruffest, tuffest, big bass sound 'bout ya, ready to bus' off your head and set you on fire."

The beat pumped even faster, faster than anything you could dance to. A flurry of snare drums echoed to the max came out of the speakers like shattering glass. 'Jungle music' the Princess thought to herself. It was so underground that none of her friends had heard of it. She felt like she was part of something really special and secret, but she just couldn't understand how anyone could dance to it. It was too fast, too mad.

Leroy had been daydreaming as he turned down the Grove. Finally, it was on. He'd have his first royal tonight; it, forgiving the pun, would be his crowning glory. And he was going to make sure he performed well also, get her begging for more. He planned to bump and grind her from all angles and keep grinding non-stop. He smiled to himself as he turned another corner. These royal women claimed their blood was blue, but like every other woman they just wanted to find a man. He had to admit that he had started becoming dazzled by the high life. This wasn't 'jungle fever', but 'red-carpet fever' he had contracted while dating the Princess. He couldn't help liking things like the solid gold dinner service at Eglington Hall, because he enjoyed lapping up the high life.

"Mmmm..." the Princess said when Leroy brushed her thighs as he shifted gear, "you're awfully good at feeling your way along... that's exactly what I need at the moment... oh God... I just want you now, desperately... desperately... desperately..."

With a screech of his tyres Leroy took the corner into Oxford Gardens so fast that he only just managed to slam the brakes on in time to avoid the police vans blocking the centre of the road outside his house.

"What the...!"

"Drive me out of here, quick!" the Princess exclaimed as she recognised the group of freelance Fleet Street photographers gathered further up. Leroy cursed loudly and shifted gear into reverse and sent the BMW into a backward lurch.

CHAPTER 12

Leroy checked the directions again. The spot should just be up this country road a bit now. He finally spotted the long, sleek Daimler limousine parked in the lay-by, next to the black Rover. Leroy pulled up beside and climbed out. He walked to the other side of his BMW and held the passenger door open for the Princess. They both climbed into the back of the Daimler, where the Prince was already sitting comfortably, engaged in doing the crossword in that morning's copy of The Times.

"I have been looking forward to seeing you," he said finally, after his initial surprise at seeing Leroy. She didn't have to explain, he guessed Leroy's identity. The black man had no business being there, but Diana had insisted...

"Have you not been looking forward to seeing me?" the Prince asked his wife.

"No," the Princess answered without emotion.

"What a pity."

The Prince was stiff upper-lip stuff, and behaved as if he was ten years older than his years. He had an overconfident attitude about him. He had never travelled by bus in his life, nor stood in a queue. He had spent every day of his life being told by family, friends and courtiers that he was the most important person in the world — after his mother — and naturally felt superior to everyone else. He certainly felt superior to his wife. The Prince felt that he had made his wife what she was today and resented her independent attitude. She had requested this meeting and when he had obliged she had brought this 'rasta man' with her.

"We just can't seem to have a reasonable conversation together, can we?" the Prince ventured. "Anyway, shall we get down to the business at hand, I think this thing needs to be resolved. Now you knew what you were doing when you married me, you ought to have got the hang of things by now. It's time to grow up, and take up your duty as future Queen of this country."

"It's an impossible situation," the Princess retorted, "I don't want to come back and I'm taking the boys with me."

"Really," the Prince said, "I can't allow that. Have you considered the implications? It would threaten the very existence of the constitution of this country which I have sworn my life to serve. If you don't return home, you will effectively lose daily access to the kids."

"You can't do that," the Princess said anxiously. "You can't do that."

"Oh yes I can. I am the Prince of Wales."

The Prince seemed cold about everything. It was clear that he did not love her at all, yet he didn't want to lose her. He turned to Leroy.

"Did you know that it is an act of treason for the Princess of Wales to be unfaithful to her husband? That means that if she commits treason her lover is committing treason as well. Did you know that England still has the death penalty for acts of treason...? But it's crazy talking about that. I'm sure you haven't yet committed treason, or have you...? It's something for you to think about."

Leroy didn't need time to think about it. The Prince was threatening him. Maybe there was some truth in what he was saying.

"All I know man, is that I don't need this. I've been thrown in jail and I've had my flat ransacked by the police, man. That's enough for me. I don't need no prince or princess in my life. This whole thing is driving me crazy."

"If you can't stand the pace get out of the race," the Prince said simply. "If you can't take the storm move along... Have you told him yet that you are just using him to get back at me?" the Prince asked.

The Princess blushed.

"What does he mean?" Leroy asked her.

"Oh it's not true... or it was at the beginning, but then I really got to like you and all that was genuine."

Leroy slapped his brow. It finally all made sense.

"So all this checking me was to get back at him? I should have known."

"Really Leroy, don't listen to him, I really did like you. I have really enjoyed our time together."

"I have come to the conclusion," the Prince began loftily, "that it really would have been easier to have two wives like my ancestors in the old days, then when one of them is giving you trouble, you simply switch to the next. Yes, I should have two wives."

"What's the point of that?" the Princess asked, "you

would only make the same mistakes as you've made with one wife but double."

"You say that I made mistakes in our marriage, but that's just your opinion."

"No, you certainly did make mistakes. You still can't understand that lack of love has always been at the root of our relationship."

"How can you say that? I gave you love... I gave you everything."

"No, you gave yourself everything. You preferred listening to opera music or watching videos in the evening, or ploughing through a mountain of paperwork to enjoying conjugal relations with your wife. Admit it, you would rather meditate for hours and chant your mantra, than spend time with me. I used to feel so lonely lying in our four poster bed waiting for you, but you would come up late and then creep upstairs when you thought I was asleep and make your way to the guest bedroom. And apart from playing with the kids, we never did anything together. You don't like my friends and I find your friends boring."

The Prince coughed nervously.

"You make it sound like all this was my fault," he said.

"Please, let's not argue now... not now," the Princess implored him. "We've gone over the situation so many times and now you're demanding a firm decision... It's just not going to happen, is it? Please be sensible."

But the Prince wasn't to be fobbed off.

"No, decide now and then we can start afresh tomorrow, otherwise we'll be in the same position tomorrow."

"I am trying to decide, but I just can't, you're holding a gun to my head. I want to be with my children, I want the best for them and I know they'll be happier if we were all happy families, but I don't know if I can be happy with you. You still think of me as the woman you married."

"I haven't thought of you like that for many years," the Prince said.

"I suppose that's a good indication of why we drifted apart."

"Do we really have to discuss this in front of this stranger?" the Prince protested again.

"He's not a stranger. He's a friend of mine, remember?"

"But why here? Are you looking for a confrontation? I don't want or need one. We should be discussing this in private."

"You never have the chance, dear. You always have some state matter or other to attend to which is more important. Nothing's more important than your woman and family," she said defiantly.

"Look you're making a spectacle of yourself, think of your position."

"And there you go again with your patronising attitude. You're so stuffy, you know that? Lighten up please, for crissakes."

The car fell silent for a moment. Then the Prince spoke slowly and deliberately.

"Look I know that our relationship hasn't been too good these last couple of years, but I'm not too proud to beg. I realise now that I need you, the country needs you and the kids need you. I don't want them to suffer

186

anymore. I want us to be a family again, and I know it can work. I'm willing to make things work. Please think about it."

"But you're threatening to deprive me of my kids one minute, telling me that you'll never grant me a divorce, and then you ask me to think about coming home! Why should I consider getting back together again when you're threatening me?"

"What am I supposed to do if I want you to stay? I've got to use any methods at my disposal. I don't have much choice about it. To not use the powers available to me would be to lose you once and for all. You have to be honest and admit that if it wasn't down to me you would have divorced me already."

"Immediately!" the Princess retorted.

"Then it's lucky for the children and lucky for our marriage that it's not down to you. I didn't make the rules dear, I only use them to the benefit of our family."

Leroy had kept quiet all this time, unable to comprehend that kings and queens had the same domestic problems as everybody else. Despite everything she said, it seemed to Leroy that the Princess was still mentally involved with her husband. He however, had had enough of playing royal escort. For all the stress he got, it wasn't worth it.

Suddenly the Princess laughed ironically.

"When we first got married, we were everybody's idea of the world's most perfect couple. How swiftly all that disappeared."

"Please dear, think of your duty, your role as mother of the future King and you've got to take it seriously."

The Princess sighed a long, deep sigh of

hopelessness. It seemed like everything was against her. 'After all I've done for that family!' she thought. She had married someone she didn't love and no longer found attractive, someone who was constantly unfaithful, but everyone including her husband felt that that didn't matter. There were other things more important than her personal questions of taste. Even though it seemed like their marriage had run its course after all these years, she had married into a thousand years of royal history and that was all there was to it. She, who was born with the proverbial silver spoon stuck firmly between her baby gums, into a family of backwater Earls — who for centuries had always been loyal supporters of the royal family and built strong ties with the Queen — was now expected to do her 'duty' for which she would be rewarded handsomely as Queen of England and if she didn't she would "effectively lose access" to her kids because of some arcane laws about heirs to the throne. If it wasn't for the kids she would have told him where to stuff his 'duty'.

"I know my duty," the Princess answered in a resigned tone, suddenly implying that she wouldn't walk out on her marriage. Being British she would maintain a stiff upper-lip as she went about her duties.

CHAPTER 13

Before the atomic age, scientists estimated that a person's worth, from a strictly chemical and material point of view, was approximately £20. In recent years, this estimation has undergone startling changes. Researchers now calculate that if the electronic energy of the hydrogen atoms in the human body could be utilised, a single person could supply the electrical needs of a large, highly industrialised country for a week. One theorist claims that the atoms in our bodies contain a potential energy charge of more than 11 million kilowatt hours per pound. In effect, the average person, by this estimate is worth roughly £50 billion over seventy years. Furthermore, trying to mechanically reproduce the human brain would cost billions of pounds. And the fact that each person is unique and unlike any other human being that has ever lived or ever will, makes them even more valuable as rarity adds to market value. Next to this natural wealth, acquired wealth looks like small change. The elders say, "a good friend is better than pocket money," but too few people realise the immense value in themselves let alone appreciate that their partners — their best friends — are more valuable than silver and gold.

Leroy had never stopped to think that Patsy was worth a lot in real terms to him. But he considered it now, realising that he couldn't live without her and it was as simple as that. As sure as he needed air to breathe, he needed her to be in his life, to be part of it, to be the mother of his children — even to be his wife. He had gone around the last few days daydreaming of a future with Patsy, trying not to think of the future without her. She had been away for a week now on one of her long haul journeys to Tokyo, San Francisco, New York and then back to London. She must have got the flowers that he had sent to each of her destinations via Interflora, and he was hoping that she would call to thank him, to curse him or whatever... just as long as he had a chance to talk to her, to explain things. She had to understand that he was a changed man. The old Leroy was gone for good.

His street vendors had noticed this also; they had never seen him like this. It was unlike Leroy not to have his mind totally focused on the pursuit of wealth. This week had been a shambles. Their requests for new deliveries had not been sorted and they had had to work with half-empty stalls. That wasn't on, they were working for a commission, not for fun. There had been some other cock-ups also, like the right order going to the wrong vendor and then the mess with the latest Beverly Hills Cop videos. On the delivery note Leroy had marked them to retail at £1.50 instead of £15! The article in The Voice that morning was the icing on the cake though. There was a picture of Leroy on the front page, handing a pair of trainers to the Rwandan ambassador under the heading: RAGGA'S INCREDIBLE

FEET FOR RWANDA!:

Kind-hearted businessman Leroy Massop, 29, has helped ease the aching feet of a hundred civil war-weary Rwandans in the strife-ridden African country by sending them each a pair of brand new trainers.

Massop, who runs a successful retail business in West London, put his money where his conscience was after being "shocked to action" by a BBC documentary about the country's bloody civil war.

"I couldn't believe the things that one black man could do to another black man in the name of his tribe," Massop said after a presentation in which the 'Mike' (sic) trainers were handed over to the Rwandan charge d'affaires in an informal ceremony at the country's embassy in London.

"We as black people are all one people and we need to sort those things out firmly — no more war! But meanwhile, we all need to play our part to help the innocent men, women and children being murdered in the Mother country."

Massop rejects claims that trainers were as high as suntan lotion on the Rwandan people's list of priorities and says he came up with his novel gesture when he noticed that most of the refugees in the documentary were barefoot.

"At least I've done something!" he hit back. "It's always the ones who sit on their backsides doing nothing who are always the first to criticise. I've also gone to my bank and paid in large cheques to the appeal. You can do that at any bank. We should all be doing that. I've done it, but I just don't need to shout about it."

By mid-morning that Tuesday the vendors had all read the article, which left them feeling more than a hint

191

of trepidation. Leroy never gave anything away for free, even a hundred pairs of sneakers which were impossible to sell. They suspected that he had been born again, because experience had taught them that when a man gave up everything he had spent his life to build up, it was usually at the call of religion.

Leroy made his way out to Gatwick Airport in good time. He couldn't afford any mistakes today, his life depended on it. Donna had given him the details of Patsy's flight. She was coming in from New York at noon. Patsy had called Donna and asked her to pick her up from the South Terminal. Leroy begged and begged and eventually Donna conceded to give him the details and leave him to do the pick-up.

"You realise that Patsy will probably kill me for doing this?" Donna said as she told him the information. "Just keep that on your conscience."

"If Patsy gets back together with me after this," Leroy promised, as he wrote down the details, "I will personally hand you the keys to my BMW convertible parked outside."

Donna smiled. The chances of Patsy giving Leroy another chance were slim, she insisted, especially as Patsy was to be in New York for a night before flying home. That would mean that she would probably be seeing J.R. there, "and you know how much he 'touches' her."

'Damn, New York, the yank!' Leroy thought. He had forgotten about that. Donna's reminder made him more determined. He had to stop this yank getting off with his woman by any means necessary.

He still had an hour to go before her flight landed, but he had decided to be out at the airport in good time. He darted in and out of the morning traffic as if his life depended on it and once on the motorway, pushed the gas pedal all the way to the ground. Now when he thought about it, he had to admit that the journey from the airport was long and it had been unfair to not offer to drive her every time she came home. If Patsy would only give him the chance, he would not only pick her up from the airport, he'd look forward to it.

He arrived at Gatwick with time to spare and quickly found a space in the car park to ease the BMW into. He thought about what he had promised Donna about the car. He hadn't really meant it, but the thought of losing his woman had taken all the pleasure out of driving the vehicle so he might as well give it away, it was only a car after all. He had come to see the BMW for what it was: an expensive pile of metal and rubber which was no substitute for the best things in life. Before he climbed out of the car, he placed that morning's issue of The Voice, with the front page turned upwards, conspicuously on the front passenger seat. It was proof to Patsy that he had changed, that nothing took precedence over her in his life.

There was a steady flow of passengers coming through from the Customs Hall, and every now and then a half a dozen tired-looking cabin crew would pass through also. Leroy was becoming increasingly nervous. He knew how Patsy stayed, she might take his being at the airport the wrong way. She might not give him a chance to make his pitch. He knew she was fully capable of giving him the big diss there and then. When he eventually saw her come through, wheeling her suitcase behind her, he smiled a huge, loving 'I've been such an idiot, please forgive me', smile and had his arms outstretched.

"What are *you* doing here?!" Patsy exclaimed when she saw him.

Leroy's face dropped, it was only then that he noticed the larger-than-life figure of J.R. Reynolds coming through beside his woman.

"Donna couldn't make it, so she asked me to do her a favour," Leroy said quickly.

Patsy kissed her teeth.

"You ask a friend to do a simple favour and she can't even do it right."

"You wanna tell me what's going on?" Leroy asked Patsy, deadly serious, his eyes staring at the American.

"Hey mac, take it easy!" J.R. warned, "that's my woman you're talking to."

"What's your problem, mate, just stay out of this..."

"Look Leroy, I don't want any trouble, okay. I ran into J.R. in New York and he happened to be coming over to England, so he decided to take the same flight. Anyway, you've got no right asking me anything, you may have forgotten but you ruled yourself out of my life. We're not seeing each other anymore, remember?"

"Yeah, you heard the lady..." J.R. said seriously.

Leroy paused, turning from Patsy to J.R., sizing up the situation. He looked around him at the crowded Arrivals Hall, with people greeting their newly-arrived friends and relatives joyfully. Why couldn't it be like that with Patsy and himself? He really didn't want to have a scene here, but he couldn't allow Patsy to go off with the yank.

"Let's just go home," he said turning to Patsy, with a pained look on his face and reaching out to take her hand.

That was his first mistake, as far as J.R. was concerned. The American threw a two-fisted combination, the first a left jab to Leroy's stomach and the second a right uppercut under his chin. But Leroy had seen the move and even as J.R. threw the first punch, moved to one side deftly. J.R.'s first punch hit an old Asian man squarely in the stomach — causing him to double up in pain. J.R. realised that he had missed with the first punch, but the second one was coming in too fast for him to hold it back. It caught the old man where it was intended for Leroy, right under the chin, sending him crashing to the ground like a nine-pin.

Patsy screamed. So did the old man's relatives who couldn't control the shock of seeing their kinsman lying on the ground cold. J.R. rubbed his right fist nervously, unable to believe what he had just done.

"Damn," he said fearfully, "Iron Mike told me that it would work."

"Police! Police!" the Asian relatives called out, trying to revive the old man.

"Hey, look I'm sorry," J.R. said anxiously, as he saw a bullet proof vested, sub-machine gun-toting policeman making his way over to the scene. "He'll be just fine... he's jus a bit dazed. I've seen a lot of boxers look like that when they couldn't take the count."

The old man started coming to, still looking groggy.

"What happened?" the policeman asked.

The old man's relatives were now hysterical and tried to explain what had happened all at once.

"Arrest this man, attempted murder. He tried to kill my father!" the Asian woman cried, pointing to J.R.

The policeman looked at J.R., then quickly slipped some handcuffs on him. He had heard enough. A basic case of assault. There were plenty of witnesses.

"Hey man, I can explain everything!!" J.R. protested.

"Save it for the magistrates, sir," the policeman said, unmoved. "Just come in from the States have you, sir? Well, guess what, you may be back there sooner than you imagined."

"Patsy!" J.R. cried desperately as the policeman led him away. "Help me!"

Leroy grabbed her arm before she could make a move.

"Leave it," he said. "There's nothing you can do. You don't want to get mixed up in something like that. Think of your job."

Patsy sighed. Leroy was right. What was done was done. J.R. would have to take the consequences. It wouldn't help if she lost her job over this. Still, it was difficult for her to turn her back, so she did so quickly.

"That will teach him, won't it," Leroy said as they made their way out the exit doors towards the car park. "I hope he's learned a lesson. He can't just come over here to England and start throwing his fists all over the place like it's a free for all."

Patsy kissed her teeth.

"Well you can talk... this is all your fault Leroy, and I'm not going to forget that. I told you not to bother me, I told you to leave me alone, didn't I? If you had listened for once, none of this would have happened."

Leroy shook his head, he thought it best not to gloat on his victory, but he was delighted that the yank had been arrested. Things had worked out beautifully. He who fights and runs away, lives to fight another day.

"So you've got yourself a bodyguard now?" he asked.

"J.R. was just trying to protect me."

"Well I hope that you both live happily ever after," he said cynically, as he crossed the road outside the terminal to the car park on the other side.

"Maybe I should have gone with him," Patsy said, "maybe at least I should help him call a lawyer. He'll need one."

"He'll be alright," Leroy insisted, "big man like that, forget about him. Any connection between that assault and you and you're fired, I'm telling you. Let's just go out and enjoy ourselves."

But that wasn't on. Patsy told Leroy to forget it and reminded him that he was history.

"We could still go out for a coffee or something," Leroy said. "Did you get the flowers?"

"What flowers?"

"I sent flowers to every hotel you were staying in, the hotel in Tokyo and the hotel in New York. You didn't get the flowers?"

"Oh those were from you?"

"Did they not have a card with them?"

"I don't know, I always sent them back."

Leroy was about to swear, but he checked himself. It wouldn't have been the right thing to do at that moment. He smiled and simply said, "What a shame."

"So did you have a nice flight?" he asked, helping her

lift the suitcase into the boot.

"Yeah, it was alright," Patsy said disinterested.

"And did you have a good time in New York?"

"Yeah I did actually. I had a really great time in New York, you know what they say, 'the city that never sleeps'."

"So good they named it twice..." Leroy added.

He unlocked her door and let her in. Patsy picked up the copy of The Voice with one hand and sat down, strapping her seat belt with the other hand.

Leroy pulled out of the car park.

"You haven't seen the latest copy of The Voice yet, have you?" Leroy asked her.

"Today's issue? Oh yeah."

Patsy opened up the paper and turned immediately to the women's pages in the centre and lost herself in reading for a moment.

"Look at the story on the front page," Leroy said eventually, realising that Patsy was engrossed in the wrong page.

She turned over to the front casually, then visually taken aback by the front page story, read it out aloud slowly as if unable to believe the words before her eyes.

"So what's all this about?" Patsy said suspiciously.

"Oh come on Patsy, can't I do something positive and get some praise for once?"

"Well in that case I'm well impressed."

"Impressed enough to give a certain attractive man, who's got a bottle of chilled Dom Perignon waiting for you at his flat, a second chance?"

Patsy looked at him then looked away, staring blankly at the road ahead. She fell silent. They hit the motorway, going back into town. Leroy slipped the gear into cruise and flexed the cramp out of his left leg before resting it.

"You heard what I said?" Leroy asked after a long while. Her silence told him she had heard. "Look gimme a break, Pat. I've been stupid, foolish, blind... yeah go ahead, whatever you want to call me. I deserve it. But look at me now, baby, I've changed. This is not the same Leroy that you last saw. This is the Leroy you once knew, that Leroy you first knew. Remember how good things used to be between us? Remember all the things we used to do together, all the places we used to travel to together and all the good times we had? Admit it, you haven't had good times like you had with me either before or after, have you? Those were some wicked times together. Those days aren't over Patsy, they're back again. And this time, nothing else gets in the way, no business deals, no money runnings. It's just me and you now, Patsy. Just say the word, please, just say the word."

Patsy sighed after a long moment.

"So... you get wise too late."

"It's never too late," Leroy countered quickly, remembering something Donna had said.

"Nevertheless, too late will be your cry. For the first thing, it's strange how suddenly you've changed to the 'old Leroy' I once knew, the moment another man shows more than a passing interest in your woman. Strange that, isn't it?"

Leroy tried to protest, but Patsy held up her hand.

"Let me finish... Secondly you've said so many times that you'll pay more attention to our relationship, that your promises aren't worth the breath they're uttered with. And finally, supposing I no longer have those feelings I once had for you when we first met, eh, the 'old Leroy' will be no good to me."

As far as Patsy was concerned, it was game set and match.

She didn't know why she had agreed to go for the coffee, but Leroy had more or less insisted that they stop off at Patisserie Claudine's, her favourite coffee shop in the West End. Leroy insisted that he wasn't trying to take advantage of her lack of resistance to the shop's irresistible French cakes. She wasn't about to admit it to him, but she had yearned for a Patisserie Claudine cake nearly all week.

They sat in the crowded bar, both sipping coffees, his a capuccino and hers an espresso and both with a large slice of cake on a saucer. Leroy remembered the first time they came to the Patisserie together. He reminded Patsy of when they used to sit amongst all the bohemian poets and painters who frequented the place and how he and Patsy used to pretend that they were black newsreader Trevor MacDonald's son and daughter so that they could get really good service or even, when Claudine herself was there, get free coffee and cakes.

Patsy laughed. She remembered it all well, how they would suddenly raise their voice and say: "Did you see Daddy reading the News at Ten on the box last night?" in exaggerated buppy voices. She reminded him of the time that Trevor MacDonald actually came into the cafe when they were in there and inexplicably continued the charade when a waitress told him that his son and daughter were also in the Patisserie. He had joined them at their table and without giving the game away, immediately started chastising his 'kids' about all the money he had wasted on them at the best public schools in the land and all they knew how to do with that education was sit in a coffee shop spending some more of his hard earned money. The whole of the coffee shop went quiet as the irate Trevor MacDonald disowned his 'children' there and then and spelt it out for them in black and white that they had been disinherited also.

Leroy was really happy to joke with his woman again, it had been a while and it was nice to have her back. He just needed the chance to roll the red carpet out. He was prepared to do anything... if she wanted sugar, he would give her sugar... He couldn't remember how long it had been since they had held each other tight, but now she had a smile on her face again, he didn't want her to lose it; he felt a need for her tonight, his lonely body was calling for attention.

Patsy didn't say yes, but at least she didn't say no. He was clutching at straws, so when she told him that she'd think about it he felt like ordering champagne for both of them in the coffee bar. She didn't want to give him back the keys to her front door and she didn't want to spend the night with him, and she didn't want to get back together again — at least not for the moment, but at least she was going to think about it.

"You know what I told Donna...?" Leroy started hesitantly, throwing in the hand he was hoping he wouldn't have to play — but what the hell. "I told her that I would give her my car, signed sealed and delivered on her doorstep if you got back together with me."

"What car, your BMW?!" Patsy asked surprised, recalling how much Leroy had dreamed about that car before and after he had bought it.

"I told her I would, so I guess I have to... You see I care about you more than I do all the material things, Patsy. I'm a changed man."

Patsy admitted that it was something she'd like to see. As they left the Patisserie she agreed to go to dinner with him the next night, just for fun.

"I'm sure you won't show up on time," she added as a passing shot as Leroy dropped her outside her Shepherd's Bush flat.

"I didn't realise I was chosen to be the future Queen of England," the Princess was saying in her private apartment at Kensington Palace, "these things don't happen by accident, but are decided on in the generations even before I was born," she said with a hint of sadness in her voice. "I was chosen to be a silent partner to the future King and because I could provide him with the necessary issue to continue his long line."

She had been spending that evening alone in Kensington Palace with her Paddington bear when she decided to call Leroy on his mobile and invite him over. It was her last night in the Palace for three months, before moving back into her husband's country mansion, where they preferred to live as a family because the air in London wasn't good for the kids. She couldn't resist inviting Leroy over.

"We've still got some unfinished business," she said on the line.

Leroy knew what that meant. He wished she hadn't called, but she had and now that he was inside her private apartments, he couldn't resist the last chance he was going to have of getting a whiff of well-trimmed and perfumed royal pussy. It would be a one off, and no one need ever know...

A call came through on the phone in the Palace apartment. The Princess picked it up.

"Oh hello Felicity... yes, I'm going off later tonight... I've decided to go back... yes I know I'm crazy, and I wish you were in my position..."

The Princess remembered something and looked up at Leroy pacing up and down.

"I'll only be a minute," she said.

Leroy looked at his Rolex, he really hoped she would only be a minute. He was aiming to get in and out fast. He had had too many experiences of the Princess' royal bodyguard to feel that he had succeeded unless he actually had the bird's bush in his hand.

To be honest, he wouldn't have gone through with this if it wasn't for curiosity. He wasn't the only man in Britain who fantasised about shagging some royal pussy but very few of them were actually going to succeed. He had the possibilities of turning those fantasies into reality, the chance to learn everything about the royal pum-pum — how deep, how wide etc. He wanted to see the Princess wheel her body and wine her bottom dressed in only a black nightie and he wanted to see her strip naked, wiggling and jiggling her stuff and he would tease her until she was crying out for a hard and stiff Jamaican wood. He would make it clear from the start that he wasn't down with no 'downtown' or '69', but if necessary, he would lick his finger to make his target sweeter, so that as the bedroom bully penetrated she would start to chat slack and cussing bad word 'bout, "Leroy, oooh Leroy, you're bad, mad and a wicked in bed..." Leroy had fantasised about giving the Princess the 'agony' so much that he could almost feel her mouth wrapped around his cock, blowing hot air gently, slowly, up and down...

However, she was still on the phone to Felicity. He wandered out into the ante-room to smoke a cigarette. The room was dark, he fumbled around carelessly in the dark. In the next instant, he heard the door slam shut. His fingers finally found the right switch and the light came on. Leroy looked around, the door seemed to have slammed shut tight. He banged on the door rapidly, but the sound of fists crashing into solid steel came bouncing back to him. There was no way out. The walls of the room were lined with solid steel and what served as the door was akin to those in bank vaults. He pounded repeatedly, but made little audible impression. He shouted out for the Princess, but his cries simply came echoing back to him. He looked around the room again and tried to figure out where he was. It was like an air raid shelter, a safe room within the Palace where the royal family could run in fear of attack, with steel-lined walls and doors and shutters that seal. Inside he found food provisions for several months, supplies of water and enough medical equipment to last for months. There was also a radio transmitter which Leroy couldn't figure out how to use. He started getting worried when he remembered that the Princess was going to be shutting up the Palace for some months. He rushed to the steel door and pounded furiously, but with no joy; the room had been designed to withstand any attack. Interestingly enough, there was a lot of reading material on the shelves including several X Press publications. Leroy sat down reluctantly to read *Single Black Female* by Yvette Richards.

...Leroy was woken by the gentle hand of Patsy.

"Hey wake up! You're going to be late for work, you know."

He rubbed the sleep slowly from his eyes and yawned a deep yawn. he looked at her and smiled with a look of relief on his face.

"Bwoy, I've had one terrible dream..."

BABY FATHER by Patrick Augustus
It takes two to tango but what happens when it's the man left holding the baby?   £5.99

COP KILLER by Donald Gorgon
When his mother is shot dead by the cops, taxi driver Lloyd Baker launches his own one man war against the police.   £4.99

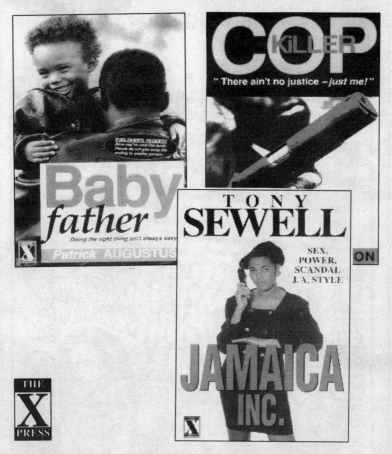

SKANK

Pure **Ragga!**

The slackest magazine...
Out every two months...£1.25

SKANK

SKANK

Pure **Ragga!**

SKANK

THE Skank

Pure Ragga!

BATTY NEW DANCE LICKS U.K.

BRITAIN'S MOST SLACK NEWSPAPER   No 1   £1.25

"SNOOP DOGGY DOG ATE MY PUSSY"

World Exclusive

SUE: MS Goldmansteiner

SCANDAL: *Snoop Doggy Dog*

Pet owner's claim shocks the world of rap music

by Mickey Berk

MURDER CHARGE rap star Snoop Doggy Dog, was dogged by more scandal last week after a Beverly Hills pet shop owner claimed the gansta rapper ate a cat in her shop.

Sheri Goldmansteiner has filed a $400 million law suit in the Los Angeles Superior court for shock trauma caused to the dead animal and loss of earnings due to the adverse media attention her shop has received.

Mrs Goldmansteiner, 68, claims the rap star, awaiting trial on a murder charge, ate the cat between two slices of bread then refused to buy the animal. "I'll sue for every dime he's got. No one comes in here and eats my pussy without paying!" She told a Skank reporter.

The rap star last week laughed off the allegations. "Ha, ha, ha, ha, ha, tee, hee... Hell that's one crazy bitch. Who's gonna believe that I'd eat a pussy belonging to some 68-year-old Jewish woman. Hell no."

BOSNIA

The scandal has caused a storm in the world of rap music with stars pledging to help clear the rapper's name.

Ice Cube is planning to personally meet President Bill Clinton this week to press the President to launch a full scale Senate investigation into the allegations.

"It's one thing to be accused of murder, but it's serious shit when you accuse a brother of eating pussy. Listen up motherfucker: that sort of thang just don't happen in Compton," Ice Cube told President Clinton in an hour long telephone call last week.

"Who's gonna believe that I'd eat pussy."

Snoop Doggy Dog

Concerned about losing the important 'rap vote' in inner city areas, Mr Clinton is likely to launch a national rap talent roadshow, clear Snoop's name, then move quickly to solve the civil war in Yugoslavia and curb the Country's huge trade deficit with Japan.

Mr Clinton is a big gansta rap fan and political pundits are predicting that he will use his planned meeting with Ice Cube to discuss whether gansta rappers could play a part in helping draft a much needed revised foreign policy in regards to the former Yugoslavia.

INSIDE: Weather, News, Horrorscopes, Crossword, Pussy, Sport

RSVP

Business-Social-Romance

EVERY CONTACT YOU'LL EVER NEED

0839 33 77 20

All calls at 36p per minute cheap rate, 48p per minute all other times.

To record your own free message or reply to one. Tel 071 359 3846

RSVP is Britain's top telephone networking club. For business contacts, romance or socialising, there's no other quite like us. To become a free member write to RSVP, 55 Broadway Market, London E8 4PH. But first check out the messages on the number above.

Moss Side
MASSIVE

By Karline Smith

"The side of Manchester few people ever get to see...wicked stuff."
VICTOR HEADLEY

"Karline Smith is an author that's certainly going places...She brings an amazing insight and human dimension to crime writing."
THE VOICE

AS baby-faced drug dealers on mountain bikes ply their trade, gun shots shatter the mid-day bustle in Moss Side, Manchester. A young gang leader lies dead on a busy road. No witnesses come forward to help the police.
THE victim's hot-headed brother, now in control of their posse's empire, swears revenge on the boss of a rival gang and his entire family. The score MUST be settled at any cost!
MEANWHILE a mother who once dreamt of 'streets paved with gold', struggles to raise her children alone in Moss Side, unaware of her eldest son's role in the killing and the gangland contract that threatens to destroy everything she lives and works for.

Single Black Female

By Yvette Richards

When thirtysomething **CAROL'S** marriage ends dramatically, she gives up on men and is convinced she'll never find happiness again.

American advertising executive **DEE** moves to London looking for new horizons and maybe 'Mr Right.'

DONNA leaves an empty relationship in Bristol and heads to the Capital in the hope of making it big as a model.

They all end up sharing a house and soon discover that black women wherever they're from, have the same problem...**MEN!**

Together they experience the ups and downs of single life in the 90's. They finally discover that something special can happen with a man when you least expect it.

Black Classics

NEW from The X Press— an exciting collection of the world's great forgotten black classic novels. Many brilliant black works of writing lie in dusty corners of libraries across the globe. Now thanks to Britain's foremost publisher of black fiction, you can discover some of these fantastic novels. Over the coming months we will be publishing many of these masterpieces which every lover of black fiction will want to collect. The first set of three books are available now!

TRADITION by Charles W Chesnutt

In the years after the American Civil War, a small town in the Deep South struggles to come to terms with the new order. Ex-slaves are now respected doctors, lawyers and powerbrokers–And the white residents don't like it one bit!

A sinister group of white supremacist businessmen see their opportunity to fan the flames of race-hate when a black man is wrongly accused of murdering a white woman. But the black population, proud and determined, strike back.

For a gifted black doctor, the events happening before him pose a huge dilemma. Should he take on the mantle of leading the black struggle in the town, or does his first responsibility lie with his wife and children?

First published in 1901 Charles W. Chesnutt's brilliantly crafted novel is grounded in the events and climate of post slavery America and the white supremacist movement. It graphically captures the mood of the period and is rightly acclaimed as one of the greats of black classic writing.

Black Classics

THE BLACKER THE BERRY
by Wallace Thurman

Emma Lou was born black. Too black for her own comfort and that of her social-climbing wannabe family. Resented by those closest to her, she runs from her small hometown to Los Angeles and then to Harlem of the 1920's, seeking her identity and an escape from the pressures of the black community.

She drifts from one loveless relationship to another in the search for herself and a place in society where prejudice towards her comes not only from whites, but from her own race!

First published in 1929, The Blacker The Berry, caused a storm when it was released. It dared to say what everyone in black America knew, but didn't want to admit. For many years it has remained a lost classic in the vault of black literature but its "raw and penetrating insight" has as much relevance for the black community today, as it did decades ago.

IOLA by Frances E.W. Harper

The beautiful Iola Leroy is duped into slavery after the death of her father but the chaos caused by the bloody American Civil War gives her the chance to snatch her freedom and start the long search for the mother whom she was separated from on the slave trader's block. With the war unfolding around her, Iola endures her hardships with a growing pride in her race. Twice she rejects the advances of a white doctor, who offers to relieve her from the "burden of blackness" by marrying her, and chooses instead to devote herself to the upliftment of her people. It's here that she eventually finds the true love she has been seeking all her life.

Iola was the most widely read black novel of the 19th century and was hugely influential in high-lighting the plight of black American slaves. It was also the first novel which featured a black woman as heroine and was an inspiration for many later black writers.